Long Shot

Beating the Odds
to Live a Jayhawk Dream

By Jeff Boschee and Mark Horvath
Foreword by Roy Williams

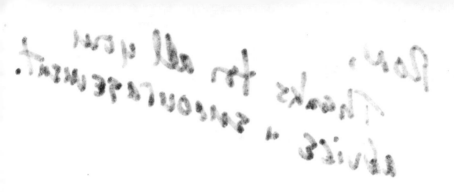

Printed in the United States of America by Mennonite Press, Inc.

ISBN 0-9725425-0-7

Cover Photo by Earl Richardson

TABLE OF CONTENTS

ACKNOWLEDGEMENTS

I would like to thank the following people for everything they have done for me. To everyone who has helped me throughout my basketball career, at every level from elementary through college, in reaching the goals I set for myself at such a young age.

First and foremost, my family. Without you, none of this would have been possible. Mom and Dad, I love you dearly. You are truly the most thoughtful and caring parents. You know how to raise a successful family. To my sister Christy, I love you. Even though we weren't the closest brother and sister, you always meant the world to me and still do. My brother Mike, what can I say? You have been my inspiration in everything I do. If Mike didn't do it, then it wasn't cool. That was my thought process. You got me started in this incredible, joyous game and I owe everything I accomplished to you.

To Markus, the main man of this book. When you asked me to do this, I was skeptical. After I met you, I knew you were a determined and trustworthy man. You made this come true and I thank you from the bottom of my heart.

To all my friends, the ones who know who I really am, thank you for supporting me in all my basketball endeavors.

To all my teammates in high school, thanks for all your work in achieving what we did.

To my college teammates, I can't say enough. You guys mean the world to me and provided me with some of the greatest thrills of my entire life. The team of 2001-02 will always hold a special place in my heart.

To all the coaches, Coach Williams, Coach Holladay, Coach Neil

Dougherty, Coach Matt Doherty, Coach Miller. You taught me so much about the game of basketball, but also were great friends.

To my high school coaches. To Coach Crutchet, thanks for having the guts to start a freshman on the varsity squad. To Coach Suko and Coach Hendrickson, I appreciate the help, knowledge and excitement you brought to the basketball season.

To the following people: Max Faulkenstein, Bob Davis, Doug Vance, Mitch Germann, Wayne Walden, Jonas Sahratian and all the managers that helped me along the way.

Finally, to all the fans who have followed me throughout my career. I can't say enough about the support you have given to me and my teammates. Kansas basketball will always have a special place in my heart. The memories that I experienced will travel with me wherever I go. The people I met, the places and cities I have visited would never have been possible without basketball. There will always be a part of me that will lie in Lawrence, Kansas.

Jeff Boschee

ACKNOWLEDGEMENTS

Any project of this size involves more than a few people whom I'd like to thank at this time.

To my family. My wife Nancy, my daughter Alison and my son Andy. I love you.

My parents, Louis and Agnes Horvath, and my brothers Tony and Dave.

Kerry Zajicek, Tom Hadt, Jim Klora, Mary Kopil, Ron Fredrick, Dave Martin, friends who filled me with encouragement.

Doug Vance & Mitch Germann, for all your help with editing this book and helping coordinate the photos.

Earl Richardson, for your generosity in opening up your personal photo gallery.

Kim Redeker, you have no idea how much your support and professional advice have meant. Once again, you've rescued a book.

Jeff Pulaski, the artist who designed this book, from front cover to the layout.

Chris McCabe, Matt VanDeursen, Jeff Sandor, athletes whose positive outlook in the face of adversity was something I used to get myself motivated.

Jeff Jacobsen, KU photographer, the man who captures the games for posterity

Matt Wieser, Joe Pellar, Collin Smith, Matt Unterfranz, Jeff Klobucar, Mike Fotia, Matt Baron, Tom Finn, Anthony Cera, Mike Wartman, Steve Egan, Jake Kocal, Robb Barbauld, Joaquin Rodriguez … thanks for being part of best basketball team I ever coached.

Jeff Boschee ... I can't begin to tell you how much I've enjoyed working with you on this book. You opened up yourself to me, and you inspired me to write. You are everything that is right with college basketball.

Thank you.

Mark Horvath

FOREWORD

When Jeff asked me to write the foreword to his book it brought back memories of writing the foreword to Jerod Haase's book "Floor Burns." Jerod's book was very touching, very emotional to read and very true and I think that Jeff's book will be the same thing. When I think of writing something for Jeff Boschee and think back on his four year career there is no question that a smile comes to my face thinking about that young man from Valley City, North Dakota.

I remember that the first time I saw Jeff, I was not even watching his game. It was at the Nike All-American camp the summer before his senior year. I was watching one game and my eyes kept drifting to another court any time there was a time out or a dead ball on my court. I kept seeing this youngster making jump shot after jump shot with the defense all over him. I told Neil Dougherty, my assistant at that time, that I was going to watch that young man that night and no one else. I remember watching the game and I found out that earlier he had scored 30 + points in the game I had watched from a distance. That night I saw Jeff score 8 points and yet he was the best player on the court. His shooting ability jumps out at you immensely, but his mental toughness is what struck me that night when I watched him play for the first time up close. The other team's entire defense was aimed at stopping Jeff and he was being "roughed up" quite a bit at every opportunity. Still, he kept getting up and coming back and that is what I remember most about Jeff Boschee's career.

For four years, Jeff was never hesitant to take the big shot and the big shot to him was the same one he took in the pre-game warm-ups. I have never coached a youngster who always made me feel so confident every time he shot the basketball. I have also never coached a young man who never shied away from the big shot and took it so nonchalantly when it went in.

Looking back on Jeff's career there is no question I will remember the jump shots. I will also remember a young man who improved drastically on the defensive end of the floor and in fact was our defensive player of the year his junior year. I will also remember a young man who handled the switch from the point guard position to the 2 guard with a great deal of grace and a young man who helped this old fella love coaching again. For four years I enjoyed Jeff and I know I will enjoy him for the rest of my life. He is a huge part of the Kansas Basketball family. I will remember the jump shots for sure and those other things too, and I will also remember that he ate more than any player I have ever coached. (Ha! Ha!)

Seriously, I think this book will give you an insight into Kansas Basketball and will give you an insight into Jeff Boschee. Perhaps it will let you get a little closer to this youngster who never changed expression, who never got too emotional, and who never gave anyone any idea what was going on inside that head. I just know he was a tough, tough competitor and he was a joy to coach. I feel very, very lucky to say he is part of my family and will be for the rest of my life. I hope you enjoy his book and I hope you will have an even greater understanding of Jeff Boschee the person.

Roy Williams
Head Basketball Coach

LONG SHOT

I think it was the way he walked onto the court that first caught my eye. There was an air of confidence about him, and it seemed too cocky for a freshman. When he played, it seemed as if he thought he was the best to ever play that position. No matter how I tried to look at him, Jeff Boschee conveyed one thing: confidence.

As his career progressed, Jeff became my focal point when watching Kansas basketball. Watching the games, I had the impression the team was going through some unusual years, and I believed the assortment of players didn't seem to fit together well. But through it all, I felt Boschee was the one constant, the link between the teams of the late 90's and the new millennium. He was the guy who arrived just as the last vestiges of the 1996-97 team were nearing graduation. He carried that tradition with him, and in my mind, was the one link to the past I had known when writing my previous book, "Floor Burns."

Years went by and I kept thinking that he would be someone who might be interested in working on another book dealing with the program I believed to be the best in America. However, this time the focus would not be on the day-to-day life of a college basketball player. This time I wanted to get into his head, to discover what gave him the confidence he projected on court. I was looking to find out how his life had progressed and brought him to this level of success.

Jeff had read "Floor Burns" as a freshman. It made introducing myself much easier, and when I contacted him a few weeks after the NCAA Final Four game, he was surprised and interested. We met in early May and began the sessions which produced this book. During the next three months, Jeff Boschee opened up his life to me.

I sincerely hope that those of you who read this book will come away with a better understanding of this enigmatic athlete. More than that, I hope the reader realizes how much hard work and determination it took for someone from a small town in a small state to make it to the national athletic stage.

Jeff Boschee could be anyone from any part of the United States. He is not tall, is not physically striking in appearance and is not the fastest person to ever play basketball. He can't dunk at will. He might not have caught the attention of many college scouts at the various camps he attended.

What he does possess is determination and character. He knew what he wanted out of his life and went after it. He set goals that seemed out of reach and then achieved those goals. He worked hard and made his dreams come true.

Along the way, he also kept his values and personality intact. Those who knew him as a ten year old still see the same person as a college athlete. The people he knew when he began his journey are still the people he treasures as his closest friends. He never forgot where he came from and is proud of that fact.

A person can be successful and still be decent to others. You can become a celebrity and not demand the spotlight be focused on your every move. There are people who realize the world does not revolve around their every whim, even though they are constantly pursued by fans who tell them a different story.

Jeff Boschee is an example of how to be all of these things. It was a long shot that a kid from a small town in North Dakota would ever be discovered and recruited by a program like Kansas. It is the 3-pointer, the "long shot," which allowed him to make his mark in the record books. In every sense of the phrase, he is truly a long shot, but one that came home a winner. Bet on it.

Mark Horvath

Chapter 1

Growing Up

BEATING THE ODDS

I used to think I could play basketball forever. The games would go on and on, there would always be a next week, and another team on the schedule. Basketball was a permanent part of my life. I guess nobody who works on this game for years ever expects it to come to an end. For me, the end of my college career came in Atlanta, on national television. In a way, the end was almost perfect. My team was behind, we needed to catch up quickly, and I found myself in a zone. The shots just flowed and there was this feeling running through me that can best be described as from another world. I just couldn't miss. My teammates got me the ball, and I started to hit every shot. It was a wonderful feeling. Everything should have been perfect.

But it wasn't. We could not catch up, and our magical season came to an end against the Maryland team who would go on to win the NCAA title two nights later. There was little comfort in that.

I left the floor after the usual opponent handshakes, following my teammates down the long corridor. I really don't remember anything specific about those first few moments. The team went into the locker room, Coach Williams said a few words, and then I sat motionless in front of my locker. The reality of what had just happened finally began to set in. It was over. My college career had come to an end.

Reporters crowded around my locker and I was asked how I felt. How do they think I feel? My career is over, my team lost in the NCAA Final Four, I believed we should have won. What else is there to say? At times like this, it's really hard to sound like a decent person. You get so mad that you want to just lash out at someone. I knew that's not what would reflect best on Kansas, and after pausing for a moment, I answered as best I could. "It's really tough to deal with this right now," I said. I don't remember what else I told the press. I went into the shower.

The entire scene leaving the Georgia Dome that night was surreal. We must have boarded a bus, but I honestly can't remember doing that. I don't even know if anyone was sitting next to me, or if I was talking with anyone. The team and coaching staff went back to our hotel, the JW Marriott, and to our rooms. I flopped on top of the bed, rolled over and put my head on the pillow, with my arms folded behind my head. Staring at the ceiling, I started to daydream....

I was back in Valley City, North Dakota, as a little kid. I must have been 5 years old when my Dad bought me my first basketball goal. It was one of those hoops you get for little kids, the ones that are 6 feet high and have a heavy piece of cardboard for the

Taking one of my first shots. Notice the form.

backboard. He put it in the family room and I would pester him until he'd play with me. "Come on Daddy, one more game," I'd say. "Jeff, this is the last one. If I win, we're going to stop playing for a while." I'd really try, taking the orange rubbery ball and trying to dribble on the floor. I'd fire up shots and feel like I was playing well. But then he'd win. So I'd throw a tantrum, yelling and insisting he play another game. If that worked (and it usually did), then I'd do it one more time. It really didn't matter to me so much that my Dad would win. After all, he was bigger. I just wanted to play more basketball. I was never going to get sick of playing this game.

I think Dad caught on after the second time I pulled this stunt. But he would always let me have my way, give me a look or a short comment, and then play me again. I must have played basketball in that family room more than I ever did in any particular gym. Sometimes I wonder what would have happened if I had never gotten that hoop.

Growing up in Valley City was great. It's a town of about 7,500 people and as a kid I can't imagine things being much better. I was never indoors. Riding my bike, swimming in the town pool and playing baseball were the kinds of things I wanted to do. Sitting inside was boring, it made me restless and that would usually end up getting my parents mad at me. Being in the house was never a lot of fun. (Unless I was playing at my indoor basketball court.) I got a job as a paper boy when I was 10 and that gave me some spending money. Looking back, it sounds like a pretty normal childhood.

I am the youngest of three children. My sister Christy is 7 years older than me, and used to always knock me around when I would tease her. In those days I was so skinny my Dad used to call me "Bones Boschee". If my sister said that, it would usually result in my teasing her until she got mad. Pretty typical stuff for a baby brother. My brother Mike is 10 years older and was the basketball member of the family. Mike was a star at Valley City High and got a scholarship to play at the University of North Dakota.

My parents were always supportive of me and encouraged me to do what I liked. To me, that meant playing basketball. Going on basketball trips began when I was in third grade. A local coach took a group of us to play games in another part of the state. Some of the best times I recall growing up were the traveling teams Valley City put together for youth basketball. My team was put together with eight of my friends from elementary school, including Dan, Nate, Lon, Digger, Austin, Matt, Kyle, and Corey.

We played in a tourney in Devils Lake, North Dakota. This was possibly the worst tournament ever held. They had referees, but each ref would stand at opposite ends of the court. They would lean up against the wall under the basket, holding a cup of coffee. While we were out on the floor, trying to play as hard as we could, they would sip from their mugs and occasionally blow the whistle. Even though we were in 5th grade, most of the guys were pretty angry at how the referees seemed not to care. I couldn't stand this. It didn't seem like basketball, it was more like somebody let the teams use their gym.

Lon Ihry and I would always polish our shoes and clean them as well as we could. We wanted to look like the college guys we watched on television and since we couldn't get new shoes, we tried to get ours as clean as possible. Sometimes the other guys would tease us, saying we were crazy, thinking someone would want us to play for their college because of our shoes. I never cared. I wanted to look my best on the floor.

As I got older, the guys would pile into a van and the coaches would drive all over the state of North Dakota to participate in tournaments. We got to stay in motels, we played against kids from places that seemed so distant, yet were only a two hours drive. I guess some of it was the fact that it made you feel so grown up, to come back and talk about going to this town and that gym with your friends.

The first time a story about me ever appeared in a newspaper, I was ten. It was an account of a game my brother Mike played during the 1990 season when the University of North Dakota made it to the NCAA Division II tournament. Somehow a reporter found out I was Mike's little brother and watched me during the game. He noticed how I cheered, how I agonized over every basket and waved my arms, trying to get the crowd to rise to their feet. The reporter wrote that although I was jubilant, yelling when Mike made crucial free throws to seal the win, my face seemed to be very stoic. (I guess that's a trait I never lost). When the Sioux won, he observed that my father and I hugged one another, happy to celebrate another victory.

He had asked me various questions during the game. I gave him short answers, trying to concentrate on the game rather than hold a conversation. I guess he thought it was because I was a ten year old, and was a bit shy. I remember that game and I know why I would not talk to the reporter. I wanted to concentrate on basketball and watch my brother. Mike taught me so much about basketball, and I never missed a chance to watch him play. I studied every move he made, I noted how the other guys on the team reacted to situations, I tried to imagine myself out there. The more I watched, the more I knew what I wanted to do. I was going to be a college basketball player.

While my father supported me in my sports activities, Mike was the one who really pushed me. He'd been there, he knew how much work it would take to become a big time basketball player, and I think he could tell how much I loved the game. He became my personal coach.

Nobody has an older brother as good as mine. Mike would take me anywhere to play ball. If there was an AAU game in Grand Forks, he'd drive me up there and sit and watch my games all day.

Driveway defense against my brother Mike.

On the way home, he'd tell me how to improve and give me advice to make me a better player. How many guys would have their little 10-year-old brother come visit at a college and leave their friends to show the kid a good time? Mike treated me as the most important person in the world when I'd come to UND (University of North Dakota). I would go on the floor with him and shoot hoops for hours. After the first time, it seemed as if I belonged out there. At least, that's how it felt to me.

Those days were helpful to me. I felt comfortable in that setting, and I think it carried over to when I began playing in junior high and high school.

Our house is actually outside of town, in a little subdivision close to the interstate highway. I would generally ride my bike to town to find other guys to play basketball. The sport was beginning to become an obsession. I'd watch games all winter on television. When I first began to play, at age 8, my favorite team was the Boston Celtics. Danny Ainge and Dennis Johnson were the pros I liked then. By the early 90's a guy from the Chicago Bulls named Michael Jordan started to become the focus of my NBA watching. It seems to me he was some bald guy who could sky at the time.

If a college game was on, chances are I'd be watching whatever team was playing. About 1992, I started watching the University of Kansas on television. The Jayhawks seemed like a cool name, and they had two guards I liked. Rex Walters was pretty good, but my favorite was Adonis Jordan. They made it to the Final Four in 1993, when the games were played in New Orleans. KU lost the Saturday afternoon game and I was disappointed. I thought if I'd gone, it might have turned out different.

The idea began to develop in my mind at that time. Maybe I could play for Kansas and be on a team like those '93 Jayhawks? If I worked hard and played basketball as much as possible, I could make it to KU. Teams always needed someone who could shoot. I was positive I could become a better shooter than I was at the time. I was 13 years old. The goal was now in front of me. I'd get myself to the point where I would be good enough to have Coach Roy Williams recruit me to be on his team. And we would get to the Final Four and win it all.

My friends started to notice how basketball obsessed I was becoming. The summers were starting to form a pattern. In the 8th grade, I began to frequent something called Noonball. This is a local phenomenon in Valley City. We have an old armory which became something like a rec center. It has enough floor space for two full courts. Every day at noon, older guys on their lunch hours from work go there to play basketball.

I shouldn't say just older guys. The ages seem to run from 18 to 50. Whoever is in the mood will just show up and the games will start. Some days they play 4 on 4, but most of the time there are at least 16-20 guys ready to play. Noonball is a year round thing, but obviously there are more guys wanting to play in the summer. That's when college students are home, and the high schools are out of session.

Games can go from 15 up to as many as 25 baskets to win. Teams are picked on the spot and it's all good natured fun. Looking back on it now, it's a very unique thing that few other towns have. We have a lot of people who love the game, want to stay in shape, and like to have fun.

The summer of '93 was when I became a regular at Noonball. I'd get some of my friends to come with me and we began a standard routine for the summer. The day began around 8 a.m. We'd go to the school and shoot around for awhile. My brother, Mike, developed a workout for me to follow. Some of the little drills included coming off screens and working on a pull up jumper. I practiced getting into the triple threat position when I would catch a pass. Eventually, I added other things I thought would be good. I made up games to make all of this more enjoyable.

We'd lift weights as well. This wasn't something my friends and I did religiously at first, but as I got older I realized how physical basketball would become. The weights became a regular part of the routine when I became a high school junior. As it got close to noon, we'd get on our bikes and head to the armory.

We were the youngest guys at Noonball. That was part of the appeal for me. Not only was I getting a chance to play ball every day against competition, but it was with guys who once played for colleges. At that age, it was a thrill and I knew it would make me a better player. If I could hold my own against these guys, I would be ready for real games against guys my own age.

After Noonball, we'd grab something to eat, wait for about a half hour and head back to play some more ball at the armory. I would want to do more drillwork, and practice my shooting and ballhandling. Often, the other guys would try to get me to stop around 3:30 p.m. or so. I'd con them into staying until closer to 5 p.m. The next morning, we'd do it all over.

I loved every minute of it. I was also trying to get to as many basketball camps as I possibly could attend. A coach from Fargo formed a team and took us to a camp at Indiana University. I played on teams that traveled North Dakota and also went to the University of Minnesota for a few days. I was testing myself against competition from anywhere.

I could not get enough of the game. Weekends usually meant playing AAU ball. I'd be traveling someplace most of the summer, playing basketball against teams from all over the state, and as I progressed, from all over the country.

It was a pretty cool way of living at the time. Being a teenager, seeing guys from cities like Philadelphia or Chicago, and being with other North Dakota basketball players was something everyone seemed to envy. They'd sit and listen to my stories, ask me things about how this place was, or how guys from some other place acted. It's pretty typical stuff for junior high and high school guys who are involved in AAU ball.

We stayed in hotel rooms and sometimes slept five guys in a room. We fought over who got the bed and who was stuck on the floor. We grew close over those months, considering how we lived and traveled. I made some pretty good friends I never would have met otherwise, since they grew up in places other than Valley City.

AAU ball is expensive as well. Parents have to be ready to spend a lot of money to pay for everything involved in this program. It's not for everyone, and the players really have to love the sport. The time involved means you will be away from home, missing out on things your friends back home will talk about often during the next school year. You almost are in a parallel world. They are getting together, dating, hanging out, going to movies and acting like typical high school kids. The basketball player is playing games in gyms, day and night. You're the same age, but your worlds will never intersect. If you want to be part of a crowd with mixed interests, it's not easy to do. Lots of guys feel left out when the school year resumes. They feel limited in what they can talk about with others who are non-athletes.

Traveling team from Valley City. Over 5 years, we were 62-6.

I loved it. I could not get enough of basketball, and the traveling was something I enjoyed. I felt I was improving all the time, my shot was getting better, I was becoming a better all around player. I kept on thinking of how this would someday lead to my being recruited by Coach Williams.

It was a dream some of my friends supported but didn't completely believe. After all, they reasoned, how many kids from North Dakota ever get seen by the major universities? I was short compared to many other guys and was still waiting to begin playing in high school. I always felt my closest friends believed in me and supported my dreams, but obviously these were long odds. I knew the chances of being recruited were slim considering where I lived. I still thought I could change things.

Scott Goffe and Jason North are two of my close friends from the Valley City high basketball team. Scott is an outgoing person, someone who can literally start up a conversation with anyone. In that sense, he is the complete opposite of me. He can be serious, but when he starts telling stories his voice becomes full of energy and he gets pretty wild. He is hilarious and has the kind of personality that makes everyone feel comfortable when they are around him. Jason is the person who could best be described as clueless. He's a great guy, funny and willing to do the most outrageous things. But there are times when he's too literal minded, and takes every thing said at face value. He gets a lot of grief from the rest of us because of that.

They were a year older than me, but were part of the summer crowd of basketball junkies I hung out with. Both of them had been periodically shaving their heads during the previous season. We all had made the varsity team and I decided to try the same type of look. I thought it would be a cool thing to do.

About the middle of my first varsity season, I went to a Target store in Fargo and bought barber shears, the kind that look like an electric razor. My hair was already cut in a flat top, so I took a pair of scissors and cut my hair down as low as possible. Using a Bic razor, I tapered the sides and back of my head, then took the shears and shaved the top as low as possible, leaving a little film of hair. The final step was to use the shears and fade in any remaining lines. My head was never shaved completely bald, and I never used a straight razor blade. I probably would have cut my scalp and missed the game.

We won that night and I had a pretty good game, scoring 11 points in my first varsity appearance against Grafton. That's when a true superstition was born. I decided that one of the reasons I had played well was the shaved head. I continued to go through the entire process before ANY game I played. It would always be the same procedure, cutting, tapering and then shaving the top. And it had to be done that day.

This meant if we were in a tournament and played three consecutive nights, I'd shave each day. If we went two weeks without a game, I would not shave until we played again. However, there was no distinction as to whether it was a game for Valley City or one of the AAU teams I played for in the summer. Game days meant shaving my head.

The University of Minnesota was one of the first colleges to contact me, actually after my sophomore year. I had played in a camp in Minneapolis that summer, and Clem Haskins, the Minnesota coach at the time, presented me with the MVP trophy when it was over. I knew I had made a good impression and almost expected them to recruit me, since they are such an overpowering presence in our state. Minnesota games and Gopher news is everywhere in North Dakota. I was hoping for a chance to play at a large Division I school, but there had to be more than Minnesota.

Obviously, the University of North Dakota tried to get me to play for them as my brother Mike had done. UND is a fine school and I would have liked to play there. At that time I was aiming for Division I and they were a D-2 school. There was one school in particular whom I hadn't heard from. I still had to figure out a way to get the attention of Kansas. I wasn't sure how, but I believed it would happen. I had to keep working at basketball, keep getting better and surely they would find out about me.

Valley City went through three different head coaches in my four years of playing there. It's one of those things that happen in a small town. The coach has a good season, looks to move to a larger school and does. It made things a bit different for me than for other guys. They knew their coaches were always going to be there, trying to get them help for college. I thought of my coaches as being good men. They were people I enjoyed playing under. However, the constant changing made getting my dream fulfilled more difficult.

By the end of my junior year, all those hours playing basketball were beginning to pay off. I was named North Dakota high school basketball player of the year, an honor at any time but almost unheard of for a junior. The papers were starting to write more stories about me and there was talk that I would be going to a Division I program out of state. Of course, nobody knew what was actually going on in my head. The only place I was interested in was Kansas. Other schools were sending me letters and coaches were starting to call me on an almost weekly basis. In the back of my mind was this voice telling me that I was hearing from some pretty good programs, but I couldn't shake the desire I had always possessed. I wanted to be a Jayhawk.

My getting noticed by Kansas meant I would have to be more aggressive. A coach from Devils Lake (a town in ND) sent a tape of me to Kansas. My AAU coach, Dave Thorsen, arranged for me to attend the Nike camp in Indianapolis. This is a select camp, by invitation only to players who are considered to be among the 200 best high schooler ballplayers in the nation. Everything I had wanted was falling into place. Now all I had to do was live up to the expectations I had set for myself.

The first day of the camp, I thought I played well. I was hitting quite a few three point shots, bringing the ball upcourt and getting my teammates involved in the offense. I noticed Coach Williams during a timeout, sitting at an adjoining court. My heart sank as I thought to myself, "he's so close but he'll never notice me." I never had time to dwell on it, as the game continued and we went on to win. Afterwards I looked over at that other court, but Coach was gone.

On the second day, we took the floor for our warmup drills, and I couldn't believe my eyes. Sitting right next to our water cooler was Coach Williams! According to the rules of the camp, he couldn't talk with me, but he smiled and watched me play for most of the day. I worked my butt off, doing everything I could at both ends of the floor. When night came, my brother Mike said to me "Jeff, you know why he was sitting at that court." "Mike," I replied "I hope you're right."

Although I kept looking, I never saw Coach again at the camp. Coach Williams later told me that when he had been watching me on the adjoining court, he asked people who I was. Someone told him, "That's the kid from North Dakota." "Well does he have a name?" Coach asked, in an exasperated tone.

The camp came to an end and I received the honor of being named one of the top 5 point guards in the camp. I had scored 40 points in one of the games, and was now being touted as one of the top 25 players in the nation. My friends Scott and Lon told me it was pretty good for a kid who was unknown outside of North Dakota a few months earlier. My brother told me to keep my head straight.

Arizona contacted me, and it was a call from Coach Lute Olson that stirred my interest in them. I heard from schools in the east, such as Furman, and southern mid-level schools as well. Indiana was still calling me, but I had no inclination to go there anymore. My only desire was Kansas.

A few days after hearing from Arizona, Coach Neil Dougherty called, asking me how I was doing and letting me know of Kansas' interest. A few days after that, I got a call I will never forget. "Hello

Jeff, this is Coach Roy Williams from Kansas," a voice said. My whole body tingled and I felt a surge of blood. I'm positive the look on my face had to be that open mouth, dumbstruck look you see on television shows. I just froze for a second. I honestly don't remember what I said in reply. I've always hoped it wasn't something lame. By the end of our conversation, Coach had pretty much offered me a scholarship to come and play for him at Kansas.

Immediately the first person I told about this was my brother Mike, followed shortly by my friend Lon. I couldn't sleep I was so excited. It was all coming true, everything I had always dreamed about.

By now, I was getting in the routine many players go through with the recruitment process. There were phone calls every day, sometimes as many as 10 or 12. Talking with coaches from schools large and small, usually about the same things. Conversations would range from "how are you playing these days?" to "we sure are looking forward to having you play for us." I'd hear about the other guys each school was recruiting, the plans for incorporating everyone into a winning team, and how much I was needed to help make this come true.

It's all very flattering. For a 16 or 17 year old, it can be over-whelming. Suddenly coaches you have seen on television for years are talking to you as if you are the most important person they have ever known. Your view of yourself takes a turn, and it's hard not to feel like you're someone special. I can easily understand how guys become arrogant. There isn't a person who is calling who doesn't try to make you feel important. How long before you start to believe it?

My brother and my friends kept me grounded in reality. They acted as if this was not a big deal. Nobody was treating me any differently than before. They would ask me about the scholarship, but I think the way they responded by not flipping out about it really helped me keep things in perspective. Mike had given me some advice that I've always felt helped me avoid getting a big head. He told me to "act like you've been there before." It's always helped keep me focused.

The KU assistant coaches started coming to some of my games. Eventually, I had to tell some of the other schools who were recruiting me of my lack of interest in their programs. This wasn't easy. Most of the coaches took it well, wished me luck and that was that. Some were a bit more belligerent. I remember an assistant coach from Marquette began to yell at me over the phone. He got quite angry and since I hadn't talked to him very often, I was puzzled by this. I tried not to say something in a smart-ass tone, and thankfully he hung up before I could.

One of the strange things about recruitment is the phone calls. They get to the ridiculous point, where coaches are telling you all kinds of things just to get you to commit. As I said, it is flattering, and I can't say I wish it never happened. It's something I'll always remember as a cool part of playing ball.

What the whole process comes down to are two simple questions: do I want to play for this man and do I want to live on this campus for the next four years? To me, those are the ultimate issues in any players' mind.

Recruiting visits are strictly controlled by the NCAA. The first time Coach Williams came to North Dakota to see me, he actually didn't speak with me. My mother and father were told they could say hello, but not actually speak with Coach. He flew in on the university Lear Jet and landed at a little air strip outside of Valley City. The high school athletic director met him and my parents met and shook hands with Coach and his wife, Wanda. According to the NCAA regulations, they could not talk with him about anything, other than to be introduced and say hello. Members of the local news media were also there to talk with Coach, but they are not allowed to specifically ask about me. All of this seems strange, but that's how it has to be performed to avoid any rules violations.

Coach and Mrs. Williams watched me work out with my brother for about 3 hours. They drove back to the airstrip and flew out. One interesting point about this trip was the fact that it was the Williams' wedding anniversary. Later, Coach told my parents this was his way of showing how much he wanted me to come to Kansas. My mother got a big kick out of that.

The second KU visit was performed by Coach Matt Doherty (now the head coach at North Carolina). Once again, he was simply there to watch me work out with my brother for about two hours. I now realize that this trip was so there would be a comparison between what the two coaches saw. They would combine each evaluation and see if there was agreement as to my skills and ability.

Next came the first time my parents could actually speak in person with Coach. In early September, both coaches, Williams and Doherty, came to my home. They brought videos about Kansas and talked with my parents and me about the program for nearly three hours. My mother made apple pie for them to eat while they were there. My mom still remembers that Coach Williams drank a few cokes, and recalled the story about how he only will drink Coke. It has to do with his childhood days, but if you look around the athletic areas at KU, you'd notice that there are only Coca Cola machines.

The final contact with my parents came when we all went to Kansas for an official visit. Again, one strange thing about the NCAA rules came into play. The Williams' had my family over to their house for a cookout. Coach Neil Dougherty and his family were also there, my first time meeting him. Since my brother Mike had come along, he was also invited to the dinner. However, the rules allow only the recruit and his parents to receive any food from the coach or staff. Thus, my brother Mike had to write a check to cover the cost of the food he ate at the Williams home. While this might sound extremely rude to some people, it was explained to us before we came, and it is proof to me of how Coach Williams does everything correctly. There was not going to be any rules infraction as far as my recruitment went, and I'm sure it's that way for every one of the guys who has been recruited by Kansas.

I decided to call Coach Williams that August and make it official. The phone call was something out of a comedy show. "Coach Williams, this is Jeff Boschee," I said. "How are you, Jeff?" he replied. I quickly got to the point. "Coach, I wanted you to know that I've decided to play for you at Kansas." "Hold on a second Jeff," Coach said. I heard the phone being put on something, then in the background there was a loud yell.

"WHOOOO YESSSS!" In the next instant, Coach Williams picked up the phone and calmly said," I'm glad you made your choice." I didn't want to laugh into the phone, but it was hilarious. I was now a Jayhawk.

That fall, I made my campus visit. Ryan Robertson was my host and he is one of the funniest individuals I've ever met. Ryan made sure I was included in everything he did that weekend, and although I realized it was part of the program, it still makes it easier for the recruit. Three other guys were also down at the same time, including Quentin Richardson, JaRon Rush and Joel Przybilla. We went to Late Night, the opening event of the basketball season. At KU, it's a night of skits by the players, a short talk from Coach, and the first official practice. The place is jammed to the rafters with fans, both students and basketball junkies from around the state. If I had been hesitant about coming to KU, Late Night sure would have clinched it. How could anyone come away from that and not believe he was in a place that loved college basketball?

Playing basketball made me into someone other than Jeff Boschee. If I were to describe myself in high school, it would be someone who was a bit of an introvert. Maybe controlled would be a better word. I was the kind of guy who would never let his real self emerge.

In many ways, that's what high school is all about. Never letting your guard down except among a few friends, never losing the image you have cultivated for yourself. The entire social structure of high school is based upon what you are rather than who you are. Labels are attached to people and that's who you become.

In my case, I was labeled a basketball star. Not a player, a star. I never thought about this too deeply at that time. I had set goals for myself and they did include some typical 14 year old dreams. I was going to break all the school records at Valley City High. I would become the all-time scoring champ, giving me bragging rights over my brother Mike. Our team would become known all over the state, and we would go on to win the State Championship.

What I never thought about was how my life would change if I actually reached these goals. It seemed to me I would remain who I was, a kid who liked to play basketball with his friends. Sure, people in my high school would know who I was without my having to become some kind of party animal. I liked the fact that popularity would follow, that when someone heard the name "Jeff Boschee" they would know who I was. Every kid who plays basketball wants the recognition. Nobody can say otherwise and be truly honest.

The surprising part of this came when letters started to arrive at my home. As Valley City began to win, as my scoring began to rise and as the publicity increased, the volume of mail started to grow. I received letters from people in cities across the state. Adults began to write to me, saying how I was a credit to the state and how I would bring recognition to North Dakota. It was strange.

Guys who were one or two years younger than I were writing to find out how I developed into an accurate shooter. They wanted to know my workouts, complete with the drills I used and for what length of time. Letters would arrive wanting to know how I developed my calves, chest and arms. Sometimes the letters would state the person went to games and simply watched my every move, hoping they could imitate and duplicate what I did on the floor. I would think about that at times. I know I never would write to someone my own age and ask advice about basketball. Yet, I must have seemed to be special if these guys were writing to me. I began to realize I had some responsibilities beyond just playing for the Hi-Liners. Maybe I was someone who would reflect upon the entire state.

After a while, I expected some of the mail to be from girls. It became obvious after my freshman year the number of girls who started to talk to me, notice me wherever I went, had increased. Of course, shaving my head all the time also caused this to happen. I can't say I didn't want the female attention, and I can't say I never expected it. The shaved head was like a beacon, and since I was getting the press, it was easy for people to know who I was. Letters from girls began to arrive but what surprised me was where they were from. Again, my basketball ability had caused my face to be shown around the state. Letters came from cities I never knew existed.

Poetry was written, there were the expected requests for pictures, autographs and dates. I was asked for advice on shooting, on school and probably other topics I can't recall. The whole process caught me by surprise.

Everyone wanted to know about me. It seemed that everyone wanted to become acquainted with me, to know my likes and dislikes, to say they were associated with Jeff Boschee. Having me as a friend across the state must have been very important. I never thought any of this would happen. Especially not in high school. It was flattering, it was overwhelming and it was unexpected.

My mother saved much of the mail I received in those years. I think she knew I would probably throw it out if it was left to me to decide. I think she also knew I would want to look at it as I grew older. It's a way to relive those times, and something few high school guys ever experience. Most people would never believe it happened at all.

My final year of high school was unforgettable. Thinking about how improbable the whole situation had been four years earlier, I guess I'm proof that dreams can come true. It made playing that senior year even more fun than before. I knew what I was doing with my future and the feeling was hard to describe. It gave me a lot of confidence.

My friend Lon Ihry moved back to Valley City before the season began, and it helped make us a better team. Lon's family moved to Valley City when we were in the 3rd grade. We actually didn't like each other at first. We would always get into shouting matches on the playground during lunch hour, especially when we played football. Eventually we found out we had a lot in common and started to hang out together.

Lon and I would spend every weekend together. We would stay the night at one another's house, playing ball, watching movies and acting like typical junior high kids. Things changed a bit when his mom got a job in Fargo. After 8th grade his family moved to West Fargo. It's only a few minutes drive between towns, so we still did a lot of things together. And then, after a series of disagreements with his high school basketball coach, Lon decided to come back to Valley City. Since his family was still in West Fargo, Lon actually lived with my family in one of our spare bedrooms. He and I finally got to play ball together during our senior year. The team was a good one for Valley City. We went 20-6 that year, and came in third in the State tournament.

I received more honors at the end of my high school career. Once again I was named North Dakota player of the year. I believe it's the only time anyone has ever received this award in both their junior and senior years. Just when I thought basketball could not have been any better for me another surprise came my way.

I was named a McDonald's High School All-American. I was thrilled to get this and amazed to hear that I was the first high school player from North Dakota to ever receive this honor. It was something I was proud of, but to my surprise, so were many people from around the state. It was as if I had helped the state gain recognition. As I got older, I realized that's exactly what happened.

As high school came to an end, there were nights when most of the guys went out to party. I went along with some friends and soon found myself in Fargo, at someone's house. We were in the basement, music was playing and people were everywhere. It's a scene that has been played out all across the country. High school kids having their senior year fun.

Quite a few of the guys were drinking. Up to that point in my life, I was a non-drinker. Basketball had taken so much of my time, and I was so dedicated to my goal of reaching KU, that I never went to many of the parties. When I did go, it was usually to see everyone and hang out. I had a girlfriend throughout high school and spent a lot of time with her. All of this combined to keep me away from some things which would have caused me to get into trouble.

On this night we were all talking above the music, laughing and enjoying ourselves. Suddenly we heard noises from above and the next moment some police officers were walking down the stairs. My heart fell into my stomach, thinking about how this would be received at home.

Leaving the floor after Valley City took 3rd in the North Dakota State Tourney my senior year.

We were given breathalyzers, and that's when I calmed down. I knew I hadn't been drinking, so I had nothing to fear. The cop who gave me the test seemed to recognize me, but I didn't know for sure. He took a few long looks at me, and when he saw I passed the test, he told me to go home. I jumped in my car and followed his advice. It's the one time I have had an encounter with the law (other than a speeding ticket), and hopefully the last.

Graduation was held on a perfect summer afternoon in 1998. As with all graduation ceremonies, we were told this was the end of so many things and the beginning of so many others. Life in North Dakota had been great, but I wanted to move on. Kansas was my dream, playing basketball was my love, and now I would get to do both. Mike had some final advice for me, and it's stuck in my mind to this day.

"Jeff, remember one thing," my brother told me. "Use basketball. Don't let basketball use you."

Chapter 2

Freshman Year

ADJUSTING

I arrived at Kansas as a typical freshman, slightly nervous but anxious to get started. My roommate was Marlon London, a guy from a suburb of Chicago. We got along, but were from different worlds and with different interests. He was a basketball player, and a good one. I liked Marlon and he made things pleasant enough. We got along well, although he was not someone who would be there if I needed someone to talk to.

Jayhawk Towers is the place where I lived. Rather than call these dorm rooms, you could say each unit is almost like a small apartment, with separate bedrooms, a small kitchen area, and a decent sized living room. Cabinets and closets are numerous enough so that a freshman would have no problem finding space for all the things brought from home. Compared to the typical KU dorm, this was a great place to live. The location is perfect for getting to classes and Allen Fieldhouse. It was no more than a ten minute walk to any of my classes, and getting to the Fieldhouse took about two minutes. I thought it was going to be a good place for me, and the people in the Towers seemed to be friendly. As the year wore on, things didn't remain that way.

Looking back on those days, I'm pretty sure people felt I was kind of cocky, especially with my shaved head and quiet demeanor. I can look at people with absolutely no expression on my face, and it doesn't mean a thing. I'm not doing it to project some attitude, it's just my nature. I've always had that kind of look. But students saw me as a Kansas basketball player, and assumed I was trying to blow them off, to act as if I was too good to speak to them. Nothing was further from the truth.

Basketball players have the same personality quirks as everyone. Not all of us are natural talkers, and we don't all love the spotlight. I know how odd that sounds coming from someone who plays in front

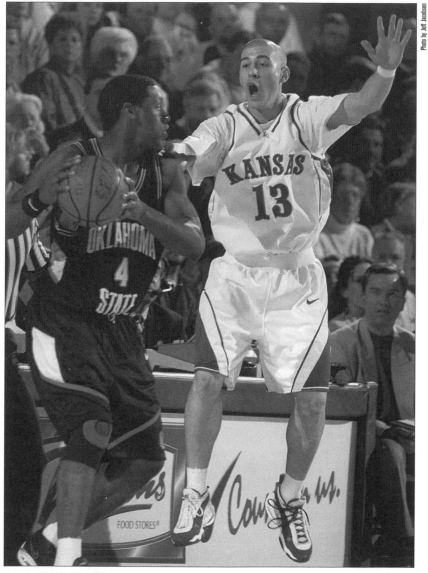

Photo by Jeff Jacobsen

I was a bald, high flyer my freshman year.

of 16,000 people on a regular basis, but it's true. Believe it or not, I'm not someone who can just shake hands and begin talking with a total stranger. It's just not me. I don't open up to people easily, and I have trouble talking with new people. Part of that comes from my father, who is a quiet man. The rest comes from not wanting to sound ridiculous. Small talk bores me, and I don't like making it. When I know someone, I can start a conversation easily, with a remark or a dig to lighten up the mood. That comes from knowing someone, and it takes me time to feel comfortable with others.

As the year went on, I noticed people starting to walk by me, looking but not saying a word. I think back and wonder if it was the shaved head. Maybe I appeared to be arrogant, as if I were someone who felt they had to draw attention to themselves. In hindsight, I probably shouldn't have kept it up when I first came to Kansas. After all, I was a freshman and should have acted the part. But I honestly felt as though I needed to keep the shaving routine, so my shooting and overall play would not be affected.

The Towers became a place of solitude, somewhere I came to study, watch TV and sleep. They were not a place for having a lot of fun. As the year wore on, basketball became the focus of my life. All I talked about, it seemed, was basketball. That was the only subject people felt they wanted to discuss. Again, there are generalizations being made that should not apply to all athletes. Actually I was almost desperate to talk about anything other than basketball.

Some nights, after a particularly bad practice or just another day when I felt really lonely, I'd come back to my room and sit. Soon, it seemed as though the walls were closing in, and the music I was listening to didn't help. I never told anyone at the time, but sometimes I'd just sit there and cry. People thought I was out all the time, laughing and partying it up, the starting freshman guard from Kansas living the good life with lots of new friends. My freshman year was completely the opposite. I have never felt so alone.

I had always kept in touch with my old friends from Valley City and now they became my lifeline. There were a lot of phone calls home to friends like Lon, Scott, and Tim. My brother Mike called me more often, sensing my loneliness and wanting to encourage me. It was a weird time. Here I was, getting all this attention from the media, having my photo on the KU website and seeing myself playing on ESPN. Yet I wanted to just sit and talk with someone about ordinary life. Most guys my age would probably say they would trade places with me in an instant. There were times that freshman year when I would have said, "Okay, let's do it now."

One of the biggest challenges a new freshman faces in college is scheduling classes. Coming from most high schools, there is no way a student is prepared to read, let alone understand, the maze of information that is called a course selection schedule. You are so accustomed to having a counselor do this for you in high school, the reality is most students are lost trying to figure things out.

This is where being a basketball player helped me. As a freshman, I was pretty much slotted into some courses which would be required of all students. It relieved some of the pressure. However, this is not always what happens.

Basketball players are not given special treatment when it comes to course selections. We are placed into something called priority registration. This means we are pre-registered into classes, usually before the other students. We can request certain times for our classes, and hope that we get into slots that meet before 3 p.m., since that's when we would have to be in the locker room before practice. For the most part, we tend to get this accomplished. It never means a non student-athlete is bumped from a course to favor one of us. It just means we get the chance to sign up for a class before most students.

However, through the years, there always seemed to be someone who did not manage to get the desired time for a course. I don't think it happened during my freshman year to anyone. In my senior season, two of the guys did not get what they wanted. As seniors, it gets harder to avoid a class which might meet during practice time. Since you are finishing up a major field of study, there might only be one section of that class. Jeff Carey had to miss Monday practices, and Brett Ballard missed Thursdays due to this situation.

Coach Williams tells everyone at the start of each season how he feels about this. In his eyes, you are here to receive an education. If that means you must miss practice one day a week, because that's the only time your course is offered, then that's how it has to be. It's not something Coach likes to deal with, but it's not as though this is a major problem. As a newcomer, this attitude pointed out to me how important it was to attend classes and get a degree.

It also showed me that I was not going to get special treatment because I happened to be on the basketball team. There is a myth in the minds of many people that athletes get everything handed to them without working as hard as other students. I can't speak for what goes on at other universities. At Kansas, an effort was made to help out the basketball team. It never meant we would get "breaks" when it came to scheduling or the grading of our work.

I remember the first time I boarded a plane at KU. I had rarely flown in my life before coming to Kansas, so there was a built in fear of what I would encounter. Of course I knew I'd be flying a lot, but that doesn't make it any easier. The type of plane we would use was something I didn't realize until one memorable day.

We generally took small planes for conference games. There were two tiny, 19 seat propeller driven planes the team used. We split up many times, and this also would accommodate managers and other personnel within the program.

I don't know what it was at first. I think the sight of the propellers threw me a bit. I remember just staring at them, thinking of those cartoon shows where someone get out and tries to spin each prop to get the plane started. I know it's ridiculous, but that's the first thing I thought about. This was already built into my mind as I prepared to be the first player to board the plane.

I walked through the open door and saw nothing. The interior of the plane was dark, and trying to peer into the rear of the plane was like looking into utter darkness. "This is some kind of omen," I thought to myself. "There is NO WAY I'm getting on this plane." I wondered if this were some kind of prank. Voices from behind told me it wasn't. "Come on, Bosch, move it," someone said. "Just find a seat and sit down."

I took that advice eagerly. I grabbed the first seat in the front. There was nothing that was going to make me sit in that black hole in the rear. For the rest of the flight I did more praying than I had done in the previous four months combined.

Jelani Janisse introduced me to college basketball. I know that sounds odd, but from a technical standpoint, it's true. Jelani was one of our guards my first season at KU. He was the strongest and definitely the quickest player I had ever seen. What made him extremely tough was the speed of his lateral moves. Jelani could cover the floor going from his left to right faster than anyone who had ever defended me in any camp or game. I could not believe how that guy could move.

We'd be working at practice and Jelani would pick me up before half court. He'd pressure me, get right on me as I was trying to see the floor and make the right decisions. Often, I'd lose concentration and make a mental error. I was struggling as a point guard and the pressure from Janisse was making it worse. Coach would get on me about this, and I knew I had to improve.

Jelani never let up. He worked my butt off every afternoon. He'd bump me, occasionally strip the ball from me, but I learned to work harder. I began to concentrate on my ball handling and developed the ability to protect the ball and keep my focus. I became a better basketball player.

Jelani never got tremendous amounts of playing time during his career. In my mind, he's one of those guys who helps a team in ways the average fan will never know. Often the guys on the bench are overlooked and fans assume they must not be very good. Nothing could be further from the truth.

Guys like Jelani Janisse contribute to the overall success of a team in so many ways. Without him applying pressure, teams like Oklahoma and Missouri would have a easy time with us every year. Young players like myself and later, Kirk Hinrich and Drew Gooden, would never develop if someone was not pressuring them in practice. We become good players because of the intensity of other good players. That's why it's called a team effort.

Some days Coach Williams really got on me at practice. He would constantly point out my mistakes, question me as to my knowledge of the game and our system, and in general, make my life hell. About mid-December, I remember Coach Williams pulling me aside and asking me how I felt about this treatment. "Coach, I'd be lying if I said I enjoyed it," I said. "Jeff," he explained, "if you can't take this, I can find another approach. I want you to understand that my goal is to make you the best player you can become."

This was another change from high school. All young basketball players talk about their coaches, sometimes with complaints, sometimes with disdain, occasionally with respect. What I was beginning to learn at Kansas was the coach is someone who is trying to make you a better player.

John Crider is a high school legend in Kansas. He's one of the all time scoring leaders in this state and has a spot in the Kansas Sports Hall of Fame, located in Abeline. John and I came to KU at the same time, a pair of shooting guards ready to take on the world. We quickly became good friends.

John was from Horton, Kansas, a small town about an hour's drive north of Lawrence. He's 6'4", with sandy brown hair, long arms and an easy smile. Like me, he also dreamed about playing for the Jayhawks. When John signed to play at KU, it was one of the biggest things that had ever happened in Horton. Imagine, a kid from a small town like Horton, population 700, having a legendary coach sign him to a college scholarship. The town closed up for a few hours, and the day was recorded for posterity in the town paper. Coach Williams drove up for the occasion, a table was set up in the school gym, crowds were in the bleachers and the local press was everywhere. John signed the letter of intent at the center circle on his high school floor, the place where he had set so many scoring records. It was like something out of a movie. John Crider was on his way to play basketball at the University of Kansas.

Crider decided to shave his head before the season began. This led to a lot of talk, both on campus and in the media. Two freshmen guards, both from small town backgrounds, both long range shooters, both with shiny white domes and wearing T-shirts under their jerseys. It was too good to be true, for those people who like to draw conclusions and form opinions without ever talking to the guys involved. We got labeled as cocky, attention grabbing kids.

Before each season Coach Williams has everyone on the team complete a 12 minute run, to see who has reported in shape for our first practices. John came in first and I was just behind him. He could really burn the track and everyone seemed pretty impressed at his speed and conditioning. Together, we two freshmen had made an immediate impact and raised a few eyebrows. Maybe it was the lack

Photo by Jeff Jacobsen

John Crider.

of hair which made us quicker.

John had one passion outside of basketball, and it was something pretty unusual. He was a mushroom hunter, someone who searched the countryside for a special type of mushroom, the Morel. These were not the garden variety mushrooms, they were large, almost the size of a football. This led to his being a member of a special organization, the name of which escapes me right now. Take my word for it, Crider was really good at finding and cooking this mushroom.

John's roommate that first year was Luke Axtell, a 6'9" shooter who was a transfer from Texas. Together with Luke, who usually wore a ten gallon hat, John would go out into the areas surrounding Lawrence every weekend in the fall or spring and hunt for mushrooms. They tried to get me involved, but this is where we parted company. I can think of a lot of things to do, but spending my afternoons hunting for mushrooms is not one of them. I did it once, but it wasn't for me.

Crider was getting some playing time that fall, but he was struggling to find himself. The shots weren't falling as much as he liked, and he seemed to be pressing. We finally got around to the first few games, the usual opening pre-season contests against traveling teams. John got into these games, but made a few errors and seemed to lack confidence. Apparently the coaching staff felt he wasn't ready, and he became a fixture on the bench. By the end of November, John was not getting into games until the final minute, if then. It began to wear on him.

John kept up a good act during this time. I knew him well enough to know how the lack of playing time was hurting him. He had pride, he believed in himself, but he felt nobody was giving him a second chance to correct his poor opening performances. The only people he really confided in were his parents.

Early in December, we had a game against Kentucky. This was the year after they had won the National Championship, and they were a pretty strong team. The game was close and we were trying to stay with them. It was at this time that Crider got his first taste of competition in almost a month.

John had been working in practice as much as anyone, but that's a lot different than getting into a big game at a critical moment. He made three errors in a few minutes and was taken out. It was virtually the last appearance of his freshman season. The coaching staff appeared to have lost confidence in him.

The season ended and John was pretty down. I could tell that he was having a hard time dealing with his season. While I had been playing, and eventually was named Freshman of the Year in the Big 12, John had suffered through the worst season of his life. I felt badly for him, because I knew if it were me, I'd be completely depressed. He had started out with a lot of hopes, but it seemed as though nothing went right for him. He was pressing, trying too hard to do things right, and eventually seemed to give up. My guess was that he would just try to put the season behind him, work all summer and try to get off to a better start his sophomore year.

Crider is the kind of guy who is a true gym rat. He would play for 6 to 7 hours a day, just shooting or getting into pickup games. He's a genuine person, not someone who puts on a mask to fit who he's with. John is a talker, with a Texas drawl that leads some people to believe that's where he grew up. He tends to say the first thing that comes into his mind, which leads to some hilarious statements. He laughs a lot, acts silly at times, and it's hard to stay in a bad mood when you are around him. All the guys on the team liked John, and we all wanted him to get his chance to play. We believed he could be a big help to the team.

Another change I noticed this first year was the amount of time I spent studying. There was no way I was prepared to make the transition from high school to college. I'm not saying that Valley City had a poor high school. I thought it was great and still do. However, there was such a huge leap for me in the quality and quantity of work I was now being assigned at Kansas. It was a real surprise.

Some of this is my own fault. I wasn't a serious student at the time and during the freshman season that didn't change. I was more concerned about my grades, but I still wouldn't say I was serious about school. There was only one priority in my life at this time and it was basketball.

I never assumed I would be "taken care of" at Kansas. Coach Williams made it very clear we were expected to be in class, doing all work assigned and getting a degree. It was never a point of discussion with him. My problem was that I was only focused on basketball, and if that wasn't on my mind, I was probably thinking about how I needed to meet some people outside of the sport.

Jeff Boschee's Galaxy began this season. I was never part of this, yet many people believed I created this place. It's actually a website devoted to me. I first heard about it from a reporter, who asked me why I had started it. The idea made me so curious I went online to check it out.

There is a photo of me in all my shaved head glory. I'm surrounded by stars and planets. Underneath the picture is information about me, including details and photos from games. When you start to read the copy, you realize I probably have nothing to do with this. At least, I would get that impression.

Others didn't see it that way. I was accused of being self-centered, of promoting without proving myself. The bad thing about the Internet is how defenseless a person is against accusations and rumors. Since it's not easy for an individual to find out who starts these sites, you almost have to grin and bear it.

It's not easy to always do this. The worst rumor that season was one stating Ryan Robertson and I were gay. The rumor intimated we were lovers. It was horrible, it was untrue, and it was almost impossible to stop. Both Ryan and I tried to figure out who and where it began, and even considered joking about it. However in the end, we just let it run its course. The less publicity and recognition we gave to this ridiculous idea, the sooner it would go away. Eventually it died, but it was pretty upsetting at the time.

There were other Internet adventures as well. Someone was pretending to be me, entering chat rooms and making all kinds of strange and lewd comments. I started to hear about this and wondered how it could be stopped.

One guy who deserves a lot of credit for my success that first season at Kansas is Ryan Robertson. It's hard to realize that he was only there for my freshman season. Ryan was the guy who taught me how to become a point guard. He showed me some little tricks, and encouraged me when I was feeling down. In hindsight, it seemed to resemble his own freshman season in many ways.

Back then, Ryan had to fill in for Jacque Vaughn, the all time assist leader at Kansas. Jacque had hurt his wrist and was out for the first ten games of the memorable 1996-97 season. It was difficult for Ryan to step in on a largely senior team, but he did it and the team went 10-0 during that stretch.

When Jacque returned, Ryan accepted his position on the bench, now relegated to a sixth man spot. He did it for the good of the team, and never thought twice about it. After that season, Ryan became the point guard for Kansas, and had two excellent seasons.

Then, in his senior year, I arrived. Suddenly he was asked again to shift positions. Now, he had to train me to become the point guard of the future, much as Vaughn had trained him. Ryan never complained. He moved to the two guard spot and became a scorer. I thought it would bother him a bit, considering how well he had performed those two previous seasons. Nothing was further from the truth.

We hung out together at times during the season and I always had a great time. Ryan was funny, he was full of energy and there was never a dull moment with him around. As a freshman, I acted as I thought a freshman should. I observed, I usually was quiet around the older guys, unless they wanted to hear from me. Ryan brought me into everything, made me more of an extrovert than I had been in college up to that time. Things were not always the best for me during that freshman year, but those moments never occurred when Robertson was around.

Ryan became my teacher. I learned so many little things from him, it's hard to detail every one. The best way to describe what he did for me is to state something I believe to be true. Ryan Robertson had a big part in my becoming a better basketball player.

One afternoon, after practice, I decided to take a walk around Allen Fieldhouse. I left our locker room, made a right turn and began to walk the track which circles the arena. As I began to get closer to the main entrance, I noticed the pictures on the walls. After spending nearly 6 months here, I finally was looking closely at the pictures which hang on both sides of the hallway.

There are photos of the many excellent teams which have played inside this historic building. Something made me look closer at the faces, almost studying the people who were on these teams. To my eyes, they seemed to be much smaller than we are today, guys who were not as physically intimidating as those I had played against thus far in my college career. I walked farther down the hall and began to see teams I remembered, the teams from the 1980's and 90's. I laughed to myself when I saw those shorts, glad that uniforms had changed over the years.

As I moved along, I realized how many All-Americans were on the walls. One side of the hallway contained pictures of coaches, including one of Coach Williams. Continuing on, I turned left, took a few steps forward and then turned left again. Once more, the walls were covered with All-Americans. Now I was seeing Paul Pierce and some other recent names. As I moved towards the lobby, the names began to go back in time, and soon the trophy cases were on my left. I stopped and looked at them.

My mind began to think about the history of this university. It struck me how many people on those walls were just names to me. I had no idea who some of them were, let alone what they had accomplished in their careers to deserve such an honor. I felt a bit embarrassed. Here I was, part of a program and a school that had produced so many great athletes yet I didn't even know many of them had existed. I had walked through this hallway many times, but until today those photos were just wall ornaments.

Kansas had always been my dream. I was now here, fulfilling my own dream and living what many other guys have wished could occur in their lives. It was still amazing to me that everything I wanted had happened. But there was so much more to come.

One of my teams could be on these walls someday. We could win a national title and have our year's banner hanging from the rafters inside the fieldhouse, above the floor. During the next three years, Kansas could produce a team everyone would remember with a smile on their face, recalling how much fun it had been to watch and cheer the Jayhawks of that season.

Then it hit me. Someday, some other guy would be walking just as I had done today. And he would probably look at that team photo with the same attitude I had felt about those old black and white pictures from the 50's. He'd probably look at our uniforms and wonder how we could have worn something that looked so ridiculous. We would be the old men who played in another era.

I stayed in the lobby for a while, just looking at everything. The yellow brick walls, the ticket booths, the view through the glass doors out to the wide lawn in front of the fieldhouse just caused me to stare. I wasn't thinking, I was just taking it all in. Someday I'd be older and bringing my own kids here to watch a game. I know they'd look at the place and see an old building. I just hope they see the history within these walls. I'd make certain they appreciate it.

That first season was pretty successful for me. I felt as though I had demonstrated why I deserved to be playing in the Big 12. I believed that I had proved a high school player from North Dakota could compete at this level, and I was feeling confident. An incident occurred in the last game of the year which was reported widely.

We were playing Kentucky in the NCAA second round. We were a heavy underdog, but suddenly everything seemed to click for us. Eric Chenowith may have played one of his best games this night, being the big presence everyone had expected from him. Ryan Robertson was getting hot and late in the game, so did I. We were into the final 10 minutes and hanging around within striking distance.

Throughout the game, Kentucky guard Wayne Turner had been trash talking. He wasn't doing it continuously, but consistently. I think a lot of it had to do with the fact that I was a freshman in a big game. He was a senior, playing on a team which had won the national title two years earlier and was given a good chance at doing it again. Turner was trying to throw me off my game. It's a form of mental warfare.

I found myself in a zone. It's one of those shooters paradise moments, when everything you throw up goes in. As Turner kept up the talk, I hit 3 three pointers in a row. The place was going crazy and I was on fire. He had just made some comment at the point where I released the ball and hit the third one. Something came over me and I turned to him and stuck out my tongue. It wasn't like a little kid, it was more of a wagging the tongue gesture. I did it to piss him off.

I ended up hitting 6 shots from 3 point range that game. We lost a thriller, 92-88 in overtime, and I went back to the hotel after the interviews were over to find myself on ESPN. I thought, "this is great, I made the highlights." It was then I realized how I was going to be portrayed. As I saw myself hitting those 3 in a row, I saw the shot of me wagging my tongue at Turner. The background voice was saying, "Not so fast, Jeff Boschee." And they proceeded to show Kentucky sealing the victory in this game.

Considering my shaved head and that gesture, it became conventional wisdom that I was a cocky freshman. I have to admit

Coach Williams taught me to learn from my mistakes and become a better basketball player.

that looking at the screen, if I didn't know myself, I probably would have come away thinking the same thing. It was very out of character for me to act that way, and most people I knew personally had fun teasing me about it. But to many KU students and fans, I was fitting their image of how I must be as a person.

Most of the team was positive after this loss because of how we fought and never gave up. We were going to be returning the entire team, minus Ryan Robertson and T.J. Pugh. We had three great recruits coming in to the program. Things were looking good that offseason.

I went into that summer confident about basketball. John Crider and I hung out most of the time. We went to our workouts together, shooting as often as possible. Being a gym rat, Crider loved having someone like me around. I had finally found someone who would not get sick of my summer pattern. We worked out a lot, went to do a few camps, and this where I first met Coach Bob Chipman from Washburn University in Topeka.

Coach Joe Holladay asked me if I would be willing to work a summer basketball camp at Washburn. I thought it would be fun and John and I found ourselves working for Coach Chip, as he's called, for a week. He's a real outgoing guy, with a great sense of humor. I enjoyed doing this so much, I kept working the Washburn camp for the remainder of my career at Kansas. Although I wasn't in his program, Coach Chipman was always encouraging, offering advice and just being there to listen if I wanted to talk basketball. It was nice to get an outside perspective on things.

John took me back to his home in Horton. His mom cooked some of the morel mushrooms the family hunted, and I have to admit they are damn good eating. They have a rich texture that gets to you if you eat too many. This is a good mushroom.

Crider also started to go out on the town with some of us that year. He had never actually drunk anything until that time. I was almost the same in that respect. This was the first year I really started to find the Lawrence night life. That summer, I'd guess we went to the bars about 3 nights a week, and we did it to socialize. With only a few summer school students around, this was where we could meet people.

Summers are when many of the basketball players catch up on course hours. The teams I have been associated with at Kansas generally found most of us taking 13-14 hours during the season. It was just too difficult to handle any more than that, and do it well. Summer was when you tried to catch up, so you could graduate on time. Since virtually the entire team stayed on campus for the summer, it was a good system. In that way, we could keep up with what we all wanted: to get our degrees and a KU diploma.

I was shopping in a Hastings store, looking for some CD's. My musical taste is truly random. I can listen to hip hop artists like Jay-Z or Nelly, but also like alternative rockers like Green Day and Foo Fighters. I have been known to put country music on my car radio and drive around with Alan Jackson or Toby Keith singing. Rock music favorites from the 80's music include Bryan Adams, Def Leppard and John Mellencamp. And there's always Aerosmith.

What caught my eye today was not a CD cover. I happened to look to my right and saw the magazine racks. On the cover of Athlon Sports was a picture of me! I was so surprised I walked over and picked up the issue. I couldn't believe it. You have no idea how it feels to see yourself on a magazine cover for the first time. I can't find the right words to express it. It's a combination of pride, shock and amazement.

I went home and called my Mom. People had apparently been calling her, telling her how they had seen my face on this magazine cover. She said she hung up the phone, immediately went to some stores in Valley City and bought some copies.

This is the kind of recognition all kids dream about. You look at these magazines for years growing up and wonder what it would feel like to see your own face on a cover. Or maybe, there will be an action shot, one of those where you are straining to make a basket or stop a defender. The thought used to cross my mind when I was 9 or 10 years old. I never thought it would actually happen.

This was the first summer when I began to wonder about basketball. I noticed how relaxed I felt, hanging out with John, taking a few classes and just having some free time for myself in the afternoons. I thought about the years in Valley City, when I played ball for 8 to 10 hours a day. It never bothered me because that was what I wanted to do.

But now I was feeling different. Was it because I was in college? Was it due to being in a larger environment like Lawrence, with Kansas City only 20 minutes away? I never worried about free time before. Why now?

My summers had always been non-stop basketball. Hell, my summer vacations were AAU trips to different gyms in various cities. Some kids had seen different sights around Chicago or Indianapolis. I knew where the gyms were. I went to camps, played Noonball, traveled with AAU, but the longest amount of time I ever went without playing basketball, in all those year, was one week.

If I didn't shoot for two days, I would feel as though my shot was starting to disappear. I constantly worked at my game. There is no doubt in my mind that all those hours are needed if a person is going to be a success and make it at the Division I level. You have to be willing to put in the time to make yourself better.

What was happening to me was something I never expected. I was now questioning how much more I was willing to do. Although I didn't realize it at the time, I think basketball burnout was beginning to develop inside of me during this summer.

Chapter 3

Sophomore Year

CROSSROADS

After my freshman year I thought the team would be a national power. We seemed to be getting our act together, and with Nick Bradford as our leader, Kenny Gregory and Eric Chenowith as our power on the floor, I figured I would contribute some points and help take pressure off the guys on the inside. Coach Williams was happy because we had added some quality freshmen in Drew Gooden, Kirk Hinrich and Nick Collison. The team was young, but infused with a lot of talent and once we learned how to play together, we were going to be great.

I began that season with more confidence than ever. I felt the freshman year had prepared me for what things would be like, and my shooting seemed to be better than ever. My ballhandling was improved, the assist-to-turnover ratio was 2:1 and I was shooting at nearly 50% from the field. I could not think of a reason why things would not be great.

On a personal note, it was a year I looked forward to with some anxiety. I had been pretty unhappy living in the Towers the first year, and I didn't see anything changing for the better. After the summer at home, I realized the biggest problem seemed my inability to adapt to living at Kansas. It's not that I was tied to home; if anything, I was happy being on my own and living in Lawrence. The town is one of the nicest places I could ever imagine. Downtown is such a great place, with restaurants, bars and shops of all kinds. It has a look that seems to have been taken from a movie. If I had to choose a college town without playing any sport, Lawrence would have been it. The problem was not living away from home, nor was it the guys on the team. The problem was in my head.

The season opening tournament was the Great Alaska Shootout, held in Anchorage, Alaska. We flew from Kansas City to Salt Lake City. From there, it was a 5 hour flight to Anchorage. I didn't enjoy it, but I sure liked what I saw when we landed.

Alaska is beautiful. Mountains surround everything. The views are spectacular and the air seemed so clear. It was like something right out of a travel brochure. As we drove into town, there was an "only in Alaska" moment. Standing right in the middle of an intersection was a large moose.

"Look at that," I said to Crider, who was next to me on the bus.

"It's goddamn Bullwinkle, waitin' for the lights to change" he replied, in that way of talking that made me laugh.

"I wish I had my gun right now," Luke Axtell said. "I'd get myself a trophy to put on my wall."

I started to laugh at the sight of cars driving around a large moose. "And these guys say I live in a remote state?" I thought to myself. The moose began to wander towards the storefronts, then went back in the direction of the intersection. This is something you'd never see anywhere but Alaska. The light changed and the bus kept on going to our hotel. For all I know that moose is still strolling around downtown Anchorage.

The day before the games began, Coach Williams arranged for us to do something unusual but memorable. As he has always done, Coach believes we should learn from our trips. He always tries to have part of a day set aside for us to either act like typical tourists, or go somewhere to experience life in the various parts of the U.S. we visit.

Today, we were going dog sledding. The team was taken to an area outside of Anchorage where we were greeted by the sight of teams of dogs, lined up in rows. The dogs were attached together by leather straps and leashed to what looked like a very large bobsled. Each sled had room for two of us ride, which kind of surprised me. I thought we would get to stand behind the dogs and tell them to "Mush," as I had seen on television. Instead, we were told to sit for the ride, with our legs outstretched in front of us. It's sort of like one of those water slide rides at an amusement part. There would be a "chauffeur" who did the actual driving of the sled.

John Crider and I decided to go together on this ride. We both sat down and looked around at the other guys.

"How the hell is Eric going to fit on any sled?" John asked.

"I know," I replied, "and look at Lester over there. He looks nervous."

"There aren't many dog sleds in the 'hood," Crider said, laughing.

The ride was not as long as I had hoped, only about 10 minutes. Those dogs can get moving faster than you would think. If I were to guess, I'd say they were moving about 15 miles per hour. The terrain is fairly smooth so there was no danger of tipping over. It was an unusual experience and something to remember from this trip.

This tournament is held in late November, so the weather was pretty cold. Of all the guys on the team, I was probably the only one who didn't find the weather too uncomfortable. Riding along in the sled, I noticed once again the beauty of the Alaskan landscape.

The only thing I didn't like about this trip was the darkness. By November, daylight is limited to about 4 hours. The sun rose each day around 11, but by 3, it was already starting to set. The amount of darkness a person must endure was something I found depressing.

The tourney itself began the following day. We played at the University of Alaska-Anchorage, in an 11,000 seat arena. It was pretty impressive and I have to admit I was surprised at the size of the place. Who would guess that basketball would be that popular in Alaska?

We won the tourney, defeating Georgia Tech in the title game. We were off to a good start, but that would change.

As the season progressed, things went wrong in a hurry. We couldn't seem to put together a sustained winning streak. We lost games we should not have lost. The fans began to get restless, and for the first and only time in my career, I heard boos directed at one individual player. It was unfortunate, but Eric Chenowith was becoming the focal point of the fans' frustration. He had a way of appearing as if he didn't care, and since he was a 7 footer, people felt he should dominate games. He didn't, and they began to lose patience.

Looking back on it, this was an unusual team. We got along well off the court. Guys would hang out, do things together and there were never any major arguments. But something happened when we got on the court. For some reason, we could not play well together. It was as if, at any given moment, someone would think they had to try and win a game on their own. Not due to selfishness, but just a feeling that they were somehow responsible for what had been happening and wanted to make things right. It led to us not always playing as a team.

I've always felt this began to drive Coach crazy. He could not figure us out, and I certainly wasn't helping. My shooting fell off as

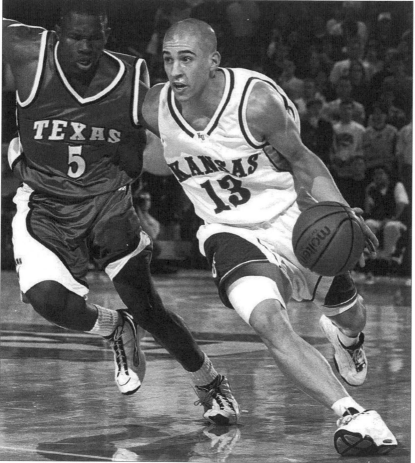

I tried to always play with intensity, the best way to earn a starting position on any team.

the season wore on and I went into a slump. I was not playing well and it began to affect me. My grades started to decline and I was generally unhappy the minute practice ended. And then, in my mind, the bottom fell out of that season.

We had been on a rare losing streak, with three bad games in a row. We lost a game at home, which is extremely unusual for Kansas. Feeling down and like we needed a change, myself, Eric, Nick and a few other guys decided to go to a bar in Lawrence. We never got drunk, and actually only had one or two drinks. We left because we were tired and it was getting late. From what I know, all of the guys went home.

The next night, on Coach Williams' weekly call-in show, a man complained, making a statement to the effect "if this team spent more time practicing and less time at the bars, they might win a few more games." Coach was taken aback by this, and assured the caller it was not something that occurred on a regular basis. The next day at practice, things weren't going well. Coach stopped practice, gathered us around at center court and began to talk. "Maybe I should start having practice at night. That might keep you guys busy. I try to believe you guys will be responsible about your behavior after games. Going out to a bar after losing a big game in this town is not smart. Have a little more pride in yourselves and make better decisions." We proceeded to have one of the hardest practices of the season.

I went home that night and realized the team had broken one of our own rules. Before each season, the seniors on the team set the rules we will follow. In my years at Kansas, the rules have never actually changed, but the seniors have the option of setting whatever rules they feel are necessary. This years team was going to have three rules:

1) Curfew will be at 1 a.m. two nights before a game. Curfew will be at midnight the night before a game.
2) No public drinking will be allowed during the season.
3) We will wear a sports coat and slacks for all pregame meals, and when we go to a game. Sports coat and tie are to be worn to dinner, but we can remove the coat if we are eating in a private room.

By going out to the bars, we had broken rule number 2. Whether or not we were drunk is not the point. We all agreed there would be no public drinking. I thought about how tough practice had been that afternoon. I flashed back to how Coach Williams seemed irritated with all of us that day. "God, am I stupid," I said aloud, although nobody was in the room. I slammed my fist down on the side of the sofa, and sat staring at the wall.

We are supposed to be representatives of the university. We certainly are a reflection of Coach and his program. The team is expected to be demonstrate a first class attitude because we are a first class program. I always felt that's what I was doing. I never thought about what I was doing that night. I guess I got so wrapped up in how poorly things were going, so involved in my own problems that I caused some new ones for Kansas basketball.

I felt terrible. There was nothing I could do about the actions of the other guys, but I didn't have to become an added burden to the problems this team was having on the floor. Causing a new situation off the court was a selfish act, and pretty juvenile for someone who wanted to be treated as a man.

There was nothing I could say to change things. I decided I would stay home from now on. As a sophomore, I wasn't sure how or what to do about this. The older guys were the team leaders. I told myself I would watch and see how they dealt with this, or if what happened dawned on them as it had on me. We wanted to make our own rules. We should have had the pride in ourselves to live by them.

It was shortly after this my low point as a Jayhawk occurred. We had been playing so poorly Coach decided it was time to shake up the lineup a bit. Along with Eric, I was benched for the following two games. It didn't mean I never got on the floor, but I didn't start and wasn't the first guy off the bench. It was extremely disheartening and I went home depressed.

"What can I do?" I said to myself. I thought about the past two years, how I had been playing fairly well but how the team had struggled at times. It wasn't exactly what I'd expected, but the problem wasn't in the games. For me, the problem was simply life at Kansas. The days were okay, but after practice time seemed to drag on forever. I realized that very few people could be called a close friend. John Crider might have been the closest, but he was wrestling with his own problems. I needed advice, someone to listen to my problems and help me out.

I called my brother Mike, the one person I knew would let me vent without making suggestions. I'm not a worrier by nature, but if I do have a problem I tend to keep it to myself. I guess I just don't think anyone else is that interested. Other times I feel it is my personal business and I should be able to deal with my problems. Most of my friends have the same attitude. We don't sit around listening to one another whine or worry. It's just the way I've lived growing up, and now that I'm an adult, I don't see much reason to change.

This time it was different. I wanted some advice and I knew Mike would give me assistance that had some intelligence behind it. He played college ball, he had lived a life similar to mine and could relate to what I was going through. The decision I placed before Mike is something I've never told anyone, not even Coach Williams. I had come to the conclusion I needed to leave Kansas and play somewhere else. It had nothing to do with the program, the fans or the other guys. It had nothing to do with being benched. The benching was part of being a ballplayer and I knew it was probably justified. Coaches have the right to make those decisions and that was not the problem.

The problem was me. I was lonely, I felt isolated and it was affecting everything I did. My grades, which were a 3.5 average in high school, were tumbling. My focus on the game was dwindling, and my performance was now being affected.

I felt like I had no close friends who were outside of basketball. Sure, the guys on the team were cool, and the times we had at practice and in the locker room were fun. Road trips were something different, and I can't say I didn't enjoy anything to do with basketball. The problem was that I didn't want to always talk about, or deal with, basketball. Having that as the main focus of my life was making me miserable, and I had nobody to get me out of that cycle. The only people I seemed to know well were basketball players. Being naturally quiet, I was not able to meet a lot of non-jock students, and as I've stated earlier, many of the students assumed I was too cocky to talk with them. I was in a box, placed there by my fame, my ability to play ball, and my personality quirk of being reserved with strangers.

Mike listened to this and told me to stick out the season. Since it was already mid-January, nothing would be accomplished by leaving. I think he hoped I'd find someone or something to get me out of this mood.

Wayne Walden is the academic advisor for the Kansas basketball program. He can arrange help for those of us who are struggling in our courses and getting tutors who will work with us. When freshman arrive on campus, he's the guy who will make the registration process easier to navigate. If it's something to do with academics, Wayne's the man to see.

I never thought I'd deal with Wayne other than a possible scheduling conflict, or possibly advice on my major. But during my sophomore year, my academics totally collapsed. I have nobody to blame for this but myself. It's not like I was under pressure and I'm not someone who worries about things. Someone who is playing college basketball has to learn how to balance the demands of classwork with travel, practices and games. It's not an easy thing for anyone to do.

At this time in my life, I simply didn't care. Everything seemed screwed up. The team was losing, I was playing poorly, I was lonely and I had enough of everything. I didn't go to class and I didn't do much work. I remember one time when I woke up and decided I would actually go to a class I had missed for two weeks. It's a good thing I did because there was a major test that day. Needless to say, I failed it miserably, but by going I didn't have to explain to anyone why I received a zero for a grade on that test.

I had never been like this in my life. My grades sunk to the worst I have ever had in my life. I had a 1.6 average that semester. This meant I would be on team academic probation. For the following semester, I would have to spend 10 hours in the Wagnon Student Athletic Center studying. I could set up the hours for whatever time of day was most convenient, but at least 2 hours every weekday had to be in study. It was going to take up a lot of time and for me, it was embarrassing. I'd never had grades this bad in my life.

(Some people might think I would be declared ineligible with grades this bad. Actually, to become academically ineligible, the NCAA says an athlete has to have a cumulative average below 1.0. This means their grades throughout their entire college career had to be this bad. One poor semester does not make someone ineligible. This is different from many high schools, and I think that's where the misconception is based. In some high schools, one F would make an athlete ineligible. Actually, it's easier to slack off at some colleges than in high school.)

The forced studying helped me get my act together. I found that I was able to get everything completed in these two hour sessions. I was able to concentrate and focus on my work. My grades improved. The program Kansas puts together for basketball players who are having grade problems works. Unfortunately, I can speak from first hand experience.

Things didn't get better. We continued to win a few, lose one. We never seemed to be a dominating team, never had the spark most Kansas teams have possessed. In some way, it was almost like a pro team that knows it might make the playoffs but knows it can't win the title. I began to get the feeling of wanting to just get this year over and start anew. I thought that whatever went wrong couldn't be fixed now, so let's just start fresh.

This does not mean I didn't want to win. It doesn't mean I didn't care. I was so frustrated with the situation I couldn't relax. I actually started to skip classes sometimes and I was starting to question my future as a basketball player, at Kansas or anywhere.

I realized I could easily dedicate myself to the game during the season. The problem was I had nothing else to do outside of basketball. That meant the summers became an extension of the season. It was as if there was never any time to just be a regular person. I was always Jeff, the basketball player, talking the game and hearing about the game. I wanted something else. I wasn't sure what it was yet, but I knew there was something missing from my life.

And then the season came to an end. We lost in the second round of the NCAA tournament and I did feel bad, worse than I had thought. I wished we could have replayed some of those games, taken back some of the errors. But we couldn't so from my point of view, I took this loss and made it an opportunity. I told myself that we could now start over and avoid the same mistakes.

If there was one thing that changed my life at Kansas, it was the arrival of help from a most unlikely source: home. My old high school friend Lon Ihry moved here. For Lon, this was a chance to get away from North Dakota. He had come for a few visits and liked the atmosphere of Lawrence. He viewed it as a new start in his life.

In that respect, it was a new beginning for me. Lon was someone who knew me as Jeff Boschee, not the Kansas basketball player. I could be myself around him, and more importantly, I did not have to talk about basketball. Most people have no idea how important that was to me at this time in my life. I needed a break from everything, and Lon's coming would offer me that chance.

In late March, right after the season ended, my old high school buddies Tim Fitzner and Jason North came down for a visit. We were driving around Lawrence, blasting some 80's metal rock tunes as loud as we could on the CD player. The car was stopped at a red light at the intersection of 23rd and Iowa, a pretty busy place. Without any warning, Jason announced, "Crank up the tunes!" He climbed out, and as the Van Halen song "Panama" was pumping out of our car, there was Jason, flailing his arms while playing a serious air guitar version, live for a captive audience. People looked at him as if he were nuts, we could not stop laughing, and every car's passengers looked to see who the two other crazy people were with this maniac.

It was a lot of fun to be this relaxed, to be myself again. For too long I had been inhibited and much of that was my own fault. I knew I should have tried to let loose, to be more of the person I always had been in Valley City. I just couldn't seem to do that unless these guys were here. They were the missing link I was looking for, the key to having complete success at Kansas.

I decided to move off campus and into an apartment with Lon as soon as the school year ended. It might be expensive, but I was going to do it. Then I got another surprise. Tim Fitzner called and said he wanted to move to Lawrence as well. Tim had been here on a few visits and fell in love with the town. He wasn't going to KU, he was going to get a job and live here. It would be like old times again, moving in with people who knew me best. I felt like I had when I first committed to Kansas. Things were going to be better from now on.

By May, I wanted to get ready for the next year. I began to use my old shooting workouts every day. I went into the weight room with renewed energy, lifting on a schedule and telling myself a season like the past one would never happen again. No matter what I did or how I did it, I would never allow any team decline as that team had. It wouldn't be easy for me to become vocal, yet I was so bummed by the whole experience I knew I would speak out if need be. I believed the nucleus of our talent was young. We had a great future if we worked hard. I convinced myself that I would have to become one of the leaders, and the best way for me to do that was to lead by example.

Another goal for the coming year was to play better than ever. The benching was so humiliating to me I never wanted to be in that situation again. Guys deal with benching in different ways. For me, it was so unexpected and so unusual it bore into my psyche. I had a hard time coming to grips with the fact that I was not starting. I realized I'd become a bit complacent and worked during the offseason to avoid that.

I was ready for my junior year. We had a good team, a strong nucleus to build upon and I felt we were going to be one of the best teams in America my final two years at Kansas.

It was at this time a bombshell was dropped on all of us in the KU basketball program. The news media was reporting that Coach Williams was going to leave Kansas to become the head coach at his alma mater, North Carolina. The story had enormous impact on every guy on the team.

Coach Williams is someone who generates enormous respect. He has no secret method, no master plan and no devious way to keep us in line. He's a real person who genuinely cares about the people in his program. I have never met anyone who treats people as honest and straightforward as Coach. He has a way of reaching inside and making his players into better people than they were when they first arrived at Kansas.

I noticed how around Coach, guys will say, "Yes sir." These are guys who would never do that with anyone else, yet it comes naturally when talking with Coach. He's almost like one of those TV dads from the old days, like Ward Cleaver on the show "Leave It To Beaver." He is proper, dresses sharp and speaks correctly without swearing.

You find yourself watching Coach Williams at work and marveling at how he does his job. He is extremely well organized, with every detail precisely stated. We have practices planned to the minute, drills beginning at 4:08 and ending at 4:14. He finds time for all of us whenever we have a question or a problem, yet never seems to slight his family or friends. He's an amazing person.

The team will go to his house at Thanksgiving for dinner. That means everyone, including the managers. He has us over at other times for brief meetings, and always has the team watching the NCAA selection show in his family room. He makes everyone feel comfortable, knowing they belong here at Kansas.

The thought of Coach leaving was something I had never considered. I was so wrapped up in my own problems that I never imagined he would consider going to another program. The news came out of the blue and was like a slap in the face. I was stunned.

Coach Williams gives me some advice during a game.

When I first heard about it, I blew it off. "This is bull. Just another attempt at creating news," I thought to myself. But then a more reliable source talked with me. My mother called and told me reporters from Chapel Hill, North Carolina, had called her, wanting a reaction to their story. They said Coach Williams had accepted a seven-year deal to become the new head coach at UNC.

In my mind the idea became a real possibility, and thoughts flashed through my head. Who might know for certain? I went over to the coaches offices and talked to CB McGrath, one of the administrative assistant coaches. He told me that Coach was considering the offer, and was actually having a tough time with the decision. Now I was concerned. He could actually be leaving Kansas.

Deep down, I had a hard time believing Coach Williams would leave. When I was recruited, he had promised me he would be there for my four years. I couldn't see him going against his word. I know it happens all the time, coaches making promises and then leaving the next year. But this was different. We were talking about Roy Williams. Doing something like that was not his style. I felt he had too much honor and decency to leave.

I was working a high school camp with Kenny Gregory when I found out about Coach's decision. Kenny had been with CB and some other people from KU. They told him Coach had made his decision and it was to stay. Kenny told me it would be on the news the following day. I was relieved, but I had never completely believed the story in the first place. After all, I believed in Coach. I knew he'd stay here because that's what he told me.

At the end of the school year a friend of mine surprised me with a gift. It was a small puppy, a West Highland White Terrier. He was white with a bit of brown fur on the edges of his ears and face. He acted so silly and made me laugh so much I named him Bozo. I love dogs and this was just what I needed. Dogs have this way of getting people out of bad moods and I certainly fit that description at the time. Playing with the pup was the perfect antidote for me. Dogs also are a great way of meeting girls. Taking the dog with me around campus, having him jump and run with those cute puppy moves, it's a cinch that women will walk up and make some comment.

Bozo, the West Highland White Terrier I received as a gift.

I kept the dog for my entire junior year and he was great to have around. Some days I would come home and just lay on the sofa, petting that dog for an hour. Bozo was part of the reason I was coming out of my funk. He helped me get my head together.

Lester Earl was the wildest teammate I've ever had. Maybe a better way to put that would be that he was a character. He was about 6'9" and everything he did was large. Lester lived life large and you could not help but get carried into his world if you were around him. Nothing he did would go unnoticed.

Lester drove a 1998 Chevy Tahoe, but it was no ordinary SUV. His vehicle had the darkest smoked windows I've ever seen. There was no possible way to see inside that car. It was outfitted with a pair of the loudest speakers anyone could possibly buy. You could hear the music if you were 4 blocks away. I once made the mistake of sitting in the back seat as a bunch of us were going to get something to eat. Lester decided to pop in a CD and the speakers started to vibrate. Suddenly I felt air blowing into my ears. Since the windows were rolled up I was puzzled at first. Then I realized that the air was actually coming from the speakers. The sub-woofers were shaking so much that they were causing the air to circulate. My eardrums began to hurt after only one block and I literally covered my ears with my hands for the rest of the ride. I had to press into my ears to relieve the pressure and deaden the sound. To Lester, it was nothing out of the ordinary. He kept on rapping to the tunes, probably thinking he had the sound down lower because I was in the back.

The Tahoe could fly. Some of the guys told me they were riding with Lester once that spring when he had the car going 75 MPH on Iowa Street in Lawrence. Since there are lights every couple of blocks, and the street itself has some hills, it had to be one wild ride. Yet, I wasn't surprised, since it was Lester doing the driving. That was his style.

Just before the end of the school year in May, Lester decided to throw a huge party. After all, what else would anyone expect from him? He called it the B.O.C., which stood for "Ballers Outta Control." Everybody on the team went, and it seemed as if one third of the campus came to this. Thinking back, this was probably the only time the entire team did any type of group bonding event that year. It was a crazy time, and it was the final event for Lester Earl as a member of the team. Let's just say he went out in his typical style. He's an unforgettable character.

Here is one of the toughest questions I've ever been asked. "What is more important to you: school or basketball?" It's a question that makes me stop and think, and there are many reasons for this.

Obviously, school is important. I can't imagine where I'd be if I had not paid attention in school and done well. The semester when I was dealing with my dilemma about staying at Kansas or leaving, my grades slipped dramatically. I felt terrible knowing what was going on, and whenever I'd get back a test or see a paper with a lousy grade on top, I felt ashamed. I knew I was capable of doing better and also knew exactly why my grades were falling. It was my fault for not working.

Taking advantage of the knowledge teachers will dispense is something that students sometimes forget. I remember back in high school, I had my friend Scott Goffe's father for a history class my junior year. He treated me no different than any other kid and was the kind of man that I think many students in our school feared. He was stern and expected you to work as well as you possibly could. However, if you did that, you would learn a great deal.

It's funny, but I also had Mr.Goffe in study hall. If someone was talking too much he would go over and empty the garbage can and put it on top of their head. As I said, he could be tough. Yet, when I would go over to Scott's house he was very different. He is a very nice man who tried not to let any of his students see his genuine side. He did care about all his students.

On the other hand, basketball is what got me to Kansas. Without the hours I spent playing the game, I never would have been able to attend this university. I look at how many places I have seen, the people I've met and the things I've experienced since I was in third grade. I would never have had those opportunities without playing basketball. No matter how good a student I might have been, getting those grades would not have helped me live the life I have had for the past ten years. I was able to live out my dreams because I could play basketball.

The final thing to consider deals with the future. Where will I be in ten years? Since there is no way anyone can know the answer to this question, it helps solve the problem of school vs. basketball. School wins the argument.

Basketball was useful the first part of my life. I know how I have felt about basketball dominating my life. I also know the odds against making it in the NBA. Consider the numbers. A 12 man roster on each of 29 NBA teams. Most of the guys are going to be playing for years. There are 29 first round draft picks who are guaranteed a contract and a spot on the team that selects them in the draft. Out of every player, from every college and university in the United States, and including foreign athletes, only 29 are sure they will play for an NBA team.

A key word is play. Will they play? Or will they receive a contract and then sit for years? When players like Karl Malone and John Stockton continue to play in their late 30's, how much time will there be for young guys? The game is still 48 minutes long in the NBA. There aren't enough minutes to go around for everyone.

I think too many young high school basketball players think NBA over education. You can name on both hands the number of guys who actually get playing time in the NBA and did not go to college. The odds are totally stacked against you. Anyone who does not think college first is crazy.

The education I've received at Kansas is going to be useful for the rest of my life. I know I made the best decision coming here. It was my dream and it came true. The fact that I've learned a great deal and have a focus on my future is a bonus I never saw as a high school senior. I'm glad I made the right choice. I think anyone playing basketball should consider everything and realize school is what counts.

Chapter 4

Junior Year
RENEWAL

One of the many changes I made at the start of this season dealt with my diet. Jonas Sahratian was a big influence in this area. Jonas was our new assistant strength coach. He's a squarely built man, probably no more than 5'10, but solid. He was someone who became involved in every aspect of our conditioning, and eating right was something he believed in. As a result, my diet became oriented towards foods which would give me energy and build up my body.

Jonas gave me a chart to follow, listing the things I should and should not eat. It contained other important information and I still have it in my apartment. The biggest change was avoiding fast food. I still could eat at some chain restaurants, but they were the types which served deli style sandwiches or non-fried foods.

This doesn't mean I'm some type of food fanatic, preaching against all that is fried. I don't religiously follow a list when I go out to eat. Actually, I discovered I enjoy most of the items and don't miss a diet full of hamburgers. My favorite food is still lasagna, and I tend to frequent Mexican restaurants. I like a steak, so I'm certainly not one of those anti-red meat people. You can offer me almost anything to eat and I'll accept.

Speaking of eating, the basketball players get a meal allowance. It runs about $525 dollars and comes in the form of a meal allowance check. The money comes from the Athletic Department's NCAA compliance office, something you would find on most, if not all, college campuses. The athlete is free to spend it on whatever food they wish to eat. Checks are issued for the entire school year, not just during the season. Because of Jonas, I have started to eat a much more healthy range of food. Yet, I never feel hungry and have a great deal more energy than in previous years.

I've learned that diet is important. My performance the final two seasons at Kansas was improved by how I was eating. I played the most minutes of anyone on the team those two seasons, and I believe part of that can be attributed to my improved diet. I was simply in great shape.

Possibly the most tragic event of my junior year occurred was when the plane carrying members of the Oklahoma State basketball team crashed. As I've said, flying is not something I enjoy. I was definitely affected by this.

We fly so much in college sports. It's almost accepted that if you are a Division I program, you will need a large part of the budget for travel. Due to the nature of sports today, games are scheduled for television and exposure. If a program is to recruit from around the nation, they must play around the nation. I never like it, but I knew I'd be in planes or airports during the winter months.

I had gone to Quintons, a deli in downtown Lawrence, with a couple of friends. We were waiting to get our food and watching SportsCenter on ESPN. As the theme music started, a weird feeling came over me. I can't explain why, but suddenly I had a very uneasy feeling, almost knowing something bad was going to open the show. Worse than that, I told one of my friends I felt the first story was going to relate to Kansas.

I found myself staring at the screen in disbelief as I listened to the details of the plane crash. At the time, no names were being mentioned as to who had survived and who had been killed. I found myself thinking about two of the guys on the Oklahoma State team I personally knew. One was a Swedish exchange student, Fredrick Jonzen, who was on my team at the Nike camp where Coach Williams had first spotted me. The other was Victor Williams, whom I had met at various camps through the summers playing ball. They were good guys, people I shared some memories with, and I wondered if they had survived. It's odd how you don't think of people for years, and suddenly news like this makes you flash back and recall things you had forgotten.

The next afternoon Coach Williams held a brief meeting before practice. He told us we were going to start traveling on one plane. We were going to be using a United 50 seat charter rather than the two, 19 seat, propeller driven planes we had been using. The coaches felt it would be wiser to be together on a single plane than risk the events which led to the tragedy.

"Don't worry about this happening to us," Coach Williams reassured me. "We're going to be positive the plane is sound before we leave. If the weather is ever questionable, we'll drive rather than fly." I felt better, although I have to admit the next few flights were pretty nerve racking for me.

For the remainder of the season, all teams in the Big 12 conference wore black velcro strips across the shoulder straps of their uniforms to memorialize the lost athletes. We had to play Oklahoma State a few weeks afterwards. I immediately went to say a few words to Victor, and felt better just seeing him and Frederick on the court. It's not that they are great friends or anything. I guess I just needed to see that life can go on after a tragedy like this.

Our fans gave each Oklahoma State starter a round of applause as they were announced. It was a way for the fans to express their sympathy and I still remember how proud it made me feel about the students and people who support Kansas basketball. Once the game began, it was as if nothing had happened. We played with as much intensity as any other game, and came away with a solid victory. But something had changed inside of me. This was one of the incidents which made me realize how unimportant basketball was compared to other things.

When we reported to practice this October, John Crider was under self-imposed pressure. He knew he had to produce quickly, or the coaching staff would relegate him to the bench for another season. His sophomore year had not gone any better than his freshman season. I was locked in to one of the starting spots, Kenny Gregory was playing the swing position, and Kirk was primed to get the other spot. John would have to become the next guy in the rotation, or he would never see the floor.

Eventually, he decided to transfer. John always wanted to play for Kansas, and the realization that he was never going to be more than one of the last guys into any game sent him into a funk. He was just not the same person I had known, and it was really sad because I couldn't do anything to help change his mood.

I relied on Crider more than he probably knew. There weren't a lot of guys I felt comfortable with that first year, and John was a soulmate. I looked forward to hanging around his room, to talking with him about subjects other than basketball. He was a good guy, and someone who really helped me adapt to life at Kansas. But I knew he was probably on his way out.

Finally, he talked with Coach Williams. John expressed his desire to play basketball, knowing it would probably not be at KU. Whatever decision the two of them made, it was something neither would talk about. This led to an incident which at the time was very controversial.

We had a home game against Fort Hays State. We built up a huge lead and Coach Williams was clearing the bench, letting everyone get some playing time. It finally got to the final four minutes of the game and everyone had been inserted except for John. The crowd started to chant " Put in Crider!" As time ticked on, the chant grew louder. "WE WANT CRIDER! WE WANT CRIDER!!" But John never got off the bench and the blowout finally came to an end.

For the next week, there were stories in papers around the state, expressing concern and at times outrage that Coach Williams would single out one player in this manner. What had Crider done to deserve this treatment? Why was he the only guy left on the bench in such an obvious situation? How could Coach Williams do this to a player he had recruited with such fanfare only two years earlier?

Nobody knew at the time what had been decided. At their conversation in late November, John and Coach had decided he would try to transfer to Washburn, a Division II school in Topeka. He would play ball there, and the size of the school would probably be more to his liking. Coach Bob Chipman was pleased to get John and agreed to keep things quiet until everything was worked out. The problem turned out to be an issue of NCAA rules. If John wanted to avoid losing a year of eligibility, he could not appear in any game for KU, even for as little as one minute. Any playing time would be considered a full year.

That's why he sat out those early blowout games. It was something that was truly difficult for John, especially hearing the fans chant his name. He wanted so badly to get on that floor and hope to change the minds of the coaches. He also knew that it was a dream, that decisions had been made and his only option was to sit and endure the final few games before his transfer became official.

The class of Coach Williams is also something I will never forget. I wonder how many coaches would take the intense criticism Coach had placed upon him, the nasty comments about his heartless and cold attitude. He never spoke about why John did not play, never jeopardized John's chances at a successful transfer. Coach let people think what they would and waited for the truth to come out. He was protecting one of his players. He showed how much he cared for every one of us, even at a time when that individual was leaving our program. I believe that in Coach Williams' mind, John will always be a Jayhawk.

I still stay in touch with John and we talked often during the Final 4 season. It seemed as though he had some regrets about leaving and missing out on the fun, the madness associated with a team getting to the last round of the NCAA tourney. He would have been one of the seniors on this team, and it would have been a memory he would never forget. We used to joke that we would stand up in each other's wedding. Knowing John's personality, I could be waiting a long time. He seems to change his mind about girls every few weeks. I know I'll never forget him, and I hope he finds the happiness he deserves. He's a good guy.

I was beginning to appreciate what I had during this season. College basketball is a unique lifestyle. We get to stay in the some of the best hotels anywhere. When I was growing up, I never would have dreamed that I would get to stay in a hotel in the heart of New York City. I would have been thrilled to be in a place with an indoor pool. This was my third year of living like this, and it certainly made me want to continue.

We eat the best food around. Our training table meal, which is held four days a week in the Burge Union building, consists of steak, chicken, salmon, vegetables, pasta, double baked potatoes, rice, fruits and juices. It's so different from just finding whatever you feel like eating, as I did in high school. I know that at smaller schools, players don't eat like we do. It's a perk and one I have to admit I enjoy. I

Kirk Hinrich and I enjoy the action on the floor.

recall that before some of the major games, we were taken out to the Hereford House, one of the best steakhouses in the nation. I am still awed by things like this. I've eaten at some places I could not believe.

Kansas plays in the best arenas in the nation. We are a top level program and that means we get to play in the top venues. I've been in the United Center in Chicago, we have played in other professional stadiums for the NCAA games, and of course, we've competed in some of the most legendary college locations in the country.

Everything we get to do is first class, top of the line. It tends to make you spoiled, expecting things to always be of this quality. If a person isn't careful, they can become arrogant about this, believing things should be their way at all times. In time, I came to realize that this was one of the benefits I had never considered when I began my career. It's part of what makes KU a great place to play basketball.

It was during the winter months that I first began to notice the change. Whenever I would walk into a room, go into a store or just stand in line waiting for something, people would stare. I thought it was pretty cool at first. "They are probably saying to themselves, 'is that Jeff Boschee?' " I thought to myself. It was very flattering to be recognized.

All that changed as time went on. It seemed to me that everywhere I went people were looking. Was I being paranoid, or worse, conceited? Did I think people had nothing better to do than look for me? I asked my friends to watch what happened as I entered places with them. Maybe they would not notice a thing, which would mean I had been exaggerating events in my mind. That's what I hoped for.

"It's just like you said," Tim told me while we were doing some shopping in downtown Lawrence. "I don't think we have entered a store where someone's head didn't turn around as soon as you walked by."

Lon added the part that bothered me. "Did you guys notice how they all seem to whisper as well? It's like they have some comment to make about Jeff, but don't want to chance being overheard."

"That would get to me after a while," Tim said.

I just gave a half laugh and kept on looking at clothes. But now the desire to shop was gone and I wanted to get back home. "Hey, let's get out of here," I suggested. "I've had enough of this for one day."

It's a natural part of being a local celebrity. It goes with being someone who is seen in the papers and on television on a regular basis. There was no way I should not have expected this type of treatment. And when I was younger, it was something my friends told me would happen. Scott Goffe used to say," Boschee you are a legend. I'm honored to be in your presence." It was always good for a laugh and he often did it to get under my skin.

I would say I'm a reluctant celebrity. Playing sports gave me a chance to get an education for free. It gave me a self-confidence I never knew I could possess. And it made my name and face recognized. That is something anyone can figure out.

What a person doesn't know is how they would handle the fame. I suppose it always seemed to me that having some athletic fame would be a cool thing. After all, how bad could it be to be well known? It was fun to pretend to be star athletes when I was shooting at the basket as a little kid. The thought that kids were now saying my name as they shot was pointed out to me once during an interview. It struck me then how powerful the success of Kansas basketball could be on our lives.

I never dreamed it would be cool for kids to pretend to be Jeff Boschee. I once received a fan letter from a mother, telling me how her son wanted to shave his head, so he would look more like me. He demanded his jersey be number 13 and was very upset when told the school never used that number. He wanted to move to North Dakota and wanted to know if he would grow to be at least 6'1". He was only 9 years old, but I was someone he admired. I was glad this came in the form of a letter. I'd probably get embarrassed if a parent told me this story face to face.

I had to learn how to deal with this. My personality wasn't ready for the attention. I liked the letters I got when I was in high school. What I couldn't seem to deal with was always being spotted, of having people stare and point at me. There are people who are already playing pro ball, people who have sold millions of CD's and people who have made three movies by the time they were my age. We are all aware that some cannot handle this intense fame. I wasn't in their league as far as fame and recognition was concerned, yet I had to find a way to handle the whispering or I would soon become a recluse.

The e-mail never stood out from any of the others. It was given a title of "Please read." There was no hint of what was inside and I might not have even opened it if the week had been busier.

Dear Jeff, I am very depressed and wanted someone to talk to. I decided to write you since I am a fan of yours. My life sucks. I hate everything about my life right now. The only time I feel good is when I watch Kansas play basketball and watch you shoot. Lately that hasn't been working either. I am thinking about what it would be like to kill myself. I don't think I could do it but I feel so lousy sometimes I want to. Write back to me so I know someone like you would care.

I sat at my computer, stunned at what I'd read. I've been getting fan mail since I was in high school. Most of the time the letters were from people who just wanted to say they wished me luck. Many were from girls, but that's another story. Occasionally I'd get some nasty letter from an anti-KU person. This was the first time I'd ever received a letter like this.

The letter made me think of how much I can influence people's lives. Basketball players are so visible compared to most other sports. The uniforms allow people to see us clearly, and reveal most of our bodies. There are no hats or helmets obscure our faces. Cameras can zoom in on us and clearly allow fans to read our lips. People sit at courtside, and it's closer to the action than any other sport. In some gyms, you can almost be touched by people from the sidelines.

Fans start to think they know us. And the sense of familiarity makes them feel as if they are also part of the team. They cry when we lose and want to run on the floor and grab us when we win. There is nothing wrong with any of this. The letter made me think about it in a different light.

I had never really thought how much good I could accomplish through my celebrity. By my talking to this person, I could literally change their life. How many other people could I help in the same manner? The possibility made me feel a sense of awe. The years I spent practicing my shot never prepared me for this. I was only concerned with becoming a better player. Now I could see how much good I could do by becoming a better person as well.

This letter had quite an impact on me. I thought about it throughout practice that afternoon. Coach Holladay had to yell at me a few times for making mental errors. At one point, he even said, "Jeff, is your mind here at all today?" I would like to have told him what was going on, but decided to keep it to myself. After practice was over, I got in my car and drove back to the apartment. My roommates were out, so I had the place to myself.

To be perfectly honest, this was one of the few times I ever worried about something. I'm not the type of person who worries about situations. Most of my friends are the same way. We tend to just say, "whatever" and go on with our lives. I know that if I really had a big problem, they might listen. This was something different.

I knew I was going to write back to this person. I just hoped these would be the right words.

Dear (name withheld), There are many things I could say but there is one thing I will tell you: you are not the only person who gets depressed. You may be surprised to learn that last year, I felt about as bad as you do right now. I was very unhappy, felt like I had no friends at Kansas, and didn't enjoy my life very much. Being a basketball player doesn't make you a special person or someone who never feels bad. Sometimes it makes things worse. I'm not an expert but I do know that things will get better for you, as they did for me. I hope this helps you out and I want you to let me know if it did.

I hit the send button and turned off the computer. There was nothing else I could do but wait and wonder if writing the letter did any good. I had no idea where this person lived. For all I knew, it could be someone I went to class with every day, or someone from back home in North Dakota.

A few weeks went by and I hadn't received a reply. To be honest, as the season progressed into late February, I forgot about the letter. I get so many e-mails a day, and was receiving so much fan mail that this letter became a thing of the past. The team was preparing for the Big 12 tourney and it was the first week of March when a reply finally came. Again, the letter caught me by surprise. It was titled the same way:

Please read. Hey Jeff, Just wanted to thank you for writing back to me. I know you are a busy person so knowing you took time to write me is pretty cool. Your letter cheered me up. So you get down at times too? I couldn't believe that. I'm glad you decided not to leave KU because you felt bad. The team needs you too much. But when I read about how you also felt bad, I realized everyone get this way sometimes. Thanks again.

I don't even know the age of this person. I'll never know where they live. To the best of my knowledge, I never received any more e-mails from them. I always will remember this event and the impact it had on me. The person said I was a great help to them. They don't know it, but their letter had a positive effect on me as well. I was starting to see the good side of being in the public eye. I could be influential in people's lives. It made me think.

The team was on a roll this season. We went into the Big 12 conference part of the schedule with only one loss. The younger guys were starting to develop as everyone had hoped. Drew Gooden began to learn the system. Unlike his freshman season, Drew listened to what the coaches were saying. He began to tailor his game to the

Photo by Earl Richardson

Kansas style, and he became a better player. As he realized this, Drew worked harder and improved quickly. It made us a stronger team.

Nick Collison also started to blossom. He became a rugged player, blocking shots and hitting the boards with authority. Nick's scoring also picked up, and his confidence level soared. Nick was never unsure of himself, but I think the other guys on the team had to see Nick actually grow into the job before their faith in him was secure.

Between the two of them, we had a presence under the boards. The missing link was Eric Chenowith. As the sophomores improved, Eric's time on the floor dwindled. He had been given every chance in the world by Coach Williams. Eric started most games, but soon saw himself taken out earlier and returned to the action later then in previous seasons. It was nothing personal and not caused by the fans displeasure at Eric's performances. The hard truth was that Drew and Nick were playing better basketball than Eric. They earned their spots and he lost his.

Kenny Gregory played the swing position. He could jump better than anyone I had seen, and was tough to guard when he went to the hoop. But his outside shot was still suspect, and it meant I had to become the shooting guard. Kirk Hinrich shared the point with me, and eventually took over the spot when I became the full time 2 guard. We were a running team, and were becoming a high scoring team as well.

We were at practice and I was playing defense when it happened. I tried to fight my way through a screen and someone hit my right hand. Instantly a pain shot up my whole arm. I shook my arm to try and relieve some of the sharp feeling, but it still tingled for a few more minutes.

It was time to do something about this. Since high school, I had been having trouble with my hand. Back in Valley City, one of my coaches was all over me in a practice, telling me I wasn't working hard enough on defense. We were doing a deny the ball drill, and I got so angry that I slapped at the ball in an exaggerated motion. I accidentally hit my hand on the offensive man's writsbone. My hand was moving in a downward motion as hit was coming up. The instant we struck one another, I felt the sharp pain go right through my arm.

It was a dumb move on my part because my inability to control my anger had resulted in hurting my hand. The pain would continue to come and go over the years. It generally took a direct hit on the hand, in just the right spot, to cause the sensation to return. But when it did, the pain was pretty intense.

I decided to have Mark Cairns, the KU trainer, look at the hand. He sent me to a specialist in town, who suggested surgery to tighten the ligaments surrounding my right thumb. Apparently, I had been playing with damaged ligaments since that day when I struck the other player, all those years ago.

The thought of surgery never scared me, since everyone seemed to think it would be relatively safe. Coach Williams had encouraged me to do it, since I would then have no worries or pain for my final season. I scheduled it for April, immediately after our season ended. Since the pain was not continuous and would not affect my play, it made sense to wait until the end of the year.

Some of the other guys were talking about injuries after practice a few days later. The comments made me think about what it would be like to have a serious injury.

I've been extremely fortunate. I've never been hurt. During my career at Kansas, I have never missed a game and have played more minutes than almost anyone else on the team. I don't know why I've been able to avoid injury. I do know that I would be completely devastated if I were to suffer a serious injury, especially one which might result in the end of my playing days.

I never wanted to be anything that wasn't somehow involved with sports. I never thought about a life without sports. I know that sounds limiting, but that's how I was, and still am. I wouldn't want to be a doctor or lawyer. Most occupations like sales would not interest me. I'd like to be a coach, preferably at the college level. My major right now is sports management, and that is about as far into the business world as I want to travel. Again, it's something involved with sports.

This surgery was not in any way going to threaten my ability to shoot or control the ball. It was performed in Lawrence on an outpatient basis in April. The recovery period was 6 weeks, and another 3 weeks of having the thumb in a splint and taking it very easy. This was the longest I had ever gone without playing basketball in my life. It had a unique effect on me, and not in a way I had anticipated.

Although I was not playing basketball, I still thought about it. However, I discovered something about myself in this period. I did not miss the game. For the first time I was able to be a normal student. I realized how much my outlook on the game had changed from where it was 10 years earlier, or for that matter, 4 years earlier.

I was truly burned out on basketball. The game didn't have the same allure for me it once did. I liked sports, but the amount of time I had to devote to being a great player just didn't seem to be worth it anymore. I found myself wanting to anything but go to the gym and shoot. I didn't want to talk about the team, the future or the sport.

Probing the defense for a weak spot

The fact that my friends and roommates were from North Dakota and not the team made this even clearer to me.

Most of the guys I grew up with never saw me as a star, or for that matter, as anyone other than the guy they had always known. They rarely talked about the games when I would come home at night, or from a road trip. Unless there was some really important fact from the game, they probably would not even mention it. Sure, they'd say "Good game, dude" or another generic comment, but we never sat down and rehashed the contents of the game. It was part of what I like about living with them. I could escape from basketball.

I was finally discovering why I needed that release. It took the injury to my hand to make me see that I was simply tired of the game, burned out on the constant exposure to basketball. The revelation made me consider my future for the first time.

My senior year was coming up. It would be played with the most talented assortment of athletes I had ever seen on my side in a contest. There was no doubt in my mind I wanted to play as good as I could this coming season. We had a chance to become the best

Tough defense means occasionally getting away with a foul.

team in America, certainly one of the top 5. It was the perfect way to end my college playing days, and if we worked hard, this team could give Coach Williams the championship we all felt he deserved. The thought of that made me feel great.

There was no lack of desire to play for Kansas next year. I could not imagine losing that opportunity. What I was deciding was the fact this would be the end of basketball for me. At the very least, I was going to take one year off from the game. The amount of work required to get into the shape for a spot on an NBA team was not something I was willing to do right now. I knew in my heart I could not devote myself to that task. I simply didn't want to play in the NBA as much as I had wanted to play for Kansas. At least, not right now.

The decision was not something that was final. Heck, nobody else knew about this anyway. I could always find out that I would get back the fire for the game. If we got to the Final Four, maybe the excitement and thrill of the experience would re-ignite the spark I once had for basketball. But it was during the summer before my senior year I came to the conclusion this would be it for awhile between me and basketball.

My decision had a real benefit for the team, although nobody would know. Unlike many college players, by not harboring any desire to go pro, I was totally committed to making my team the best it could be. I would not be distracted by any other thoughts, by the possibility of needing to get an agent or any other thing associated with turning pro. I could be a team leader with only one goal: the team itself.

The season came to an end in the Sweet 16 round of the NCAA tournament. Illinois, the Big Ten champion, was a team on fire at the right time and we simply could not match up against them. Losing this game was not as bad as what was said about us afterwards.

Illinois was a big, physical team, one that was well suited for the style of play found in the Big Ten. It's a conference that prides itself on playing a rough game, not finesse or speed but brute force. We knew that coming into the game, but we just could not get our shots to fall. They were the better team that day and they deserved to win.

I could live with any assessment of our loss except the one the press decided to present. Losing was one thing, but being declared soft and afraid was quite another. Our team might have lost this game, but we certainly were not afraid. Illinois hit the boards better than we did in this game. They have a great front line and loads of talent. I would never take anything away from their ability.

However, I was very angry at the comments made about Kansas. It was as if people were trying to knock us because we have been so successful for so many years. They can't take away the conference championships and tourney victories, so they find another way to try and tarnish our reputation. Labeling us "soft" makes us look like wimps. It's the kind of thing that strikes me as a personal attack rather than one based on some analysis of our game. It hurt and was very unfair.

The comments also served to motivate many of the guys. We had always worked out in the offseason, but there seemed to be more intensity during the summer after the Illinois loss. I know I was much more serious when I entered the weight room. There were times when I wondered why it bothered me so much. After all, it's not as though I had been challenged to a fight or something. Yet, it seemed as though the national press was questioning our manhood, our toughness and our desire.

I knew we would never again be the team caught off guard by a physical team. If we ever played Illinois again, I had the feeling we would be almost too rough, and that could get us in foul trouble. Yet, I almost welcomed the thought. If we were to push and shove a physical team around, would they start calling us "dirty players?"

Final Four Team. The 2001-2002 University of Kansas Jayhawks.

Chapter 5

Senior Year

BEGINNINGS

My final season began with the usual predictions. We were supposed to be contending for the Big 12 title, and some people said we could make it far into the NCAA tourney. Nobody was predicting a Final Four finish. Kansas had the recent history of folding in the early rounds, deserved or not. Since this team was viewed as being young, perhaps a year away, getting as far as we did was just not in the cards. Not this year anyway.

Each year we have guys who are designated team captains. It's an honor which goes to seniors who have played in the program for three years. In their senior year, they are listed as co-captains. This year Jeff Carey and I were selected for this honor. Being captain of the Kansas Jayhawks is a recognition I will treasure and am proud to have held. When I think of past captains, I realize I'm truly in the company of some great players.

The position is one molded by the individuals who hold it. Season to season, captains create a mood for a team, an atmosphere through which practices, locker room situations, traveling and pre-game attitudes are affected. The captain sets the tone for an entire season. Many times the guys on the team don't even realize this until the year is done and there is time to reflect.

If the captain is someone who takes things casually, who acts as though things aren't important, the team picks that up. Captains who seem to convey a specific feeling about the coaching staff can also signal how the rest of the team will respond. It's strange how we adapt to who holds the title of captain. Looking at the setup of a college team, obviously the coach has the power. Guys were recruited for a purpose and the captain can't change how the coach judges talent and how to utilize it. It's not a 7th grade pickup game, where captains dictate who plays and who sits.

Why do we have captains? If the team knows what to do, and is composed of mature young adults with a successful coach, what possible reason is there for choosing a captain?

I felt as though I was a leader while being captain. I'm not a loud person during games or practices. I'm the type of person who prefers to lead by example rather than shouting words. You have to be able to perform, to demonstrate a style you want the rest of the guys to pick up. I've always felt more respect for guys who simply played their butts off anytime they were on the floor than those who talked about it. My attitude is back up what you say.

Fans have told me they never seem to see me talking during games. My mouth is not moving much and there are very few photos of me with my veins popping out in my neck, screaming at my teammates during a game. It's just not something I've ever done. But there was one occasion this year when I yelled during a game.

We were playing Iowa State. Things weren't going well and I had just about had enough. As we were coming into a huddle, I yelled, "Let's f---ing Go!" It was so out of character that Keith Langford was completely shocked. After the game, Keith said he was so startled by what I said, and how I said it, that he was all pumped up. He played one of his best halves of the year that night.

This may come as a surprise to some people, but I don't always hang out with the guys on the team. We get along well, and I honestly believe that we're a close team. But close doesn't mean always together. Close means we respect one another as players, are unselfish on the court and like each other as people. That's where it ends.

Some guys feel that basketball is life. (There is a T-shirt with that slogan emblazoned on the front.) It's not. It's a game that can give you many good times, a game that is the greatest ever invented. For someone who wants to make it their life, the statement is true.

I've always found that to be a weird slogan. I can't live that way, and I believe it's why I got burned out on basketball. I used to eat, sleep and drink basketball. It seemed to be strangling me, and it was very limiting. I think it's like anything else a person does in life. Balance things out. You need to add a little spice to your life. Do other things besides basketball.

In no way am I trying to diminish the importance of teams. The guys on the team are great people. Nick Collison is one of the funniest people I've known, able to get off a wisecrack at any time. Nick is the type of guy you can't always take seriously. He likes to throw out one-liners, usually to loosen up the mood in the locker room. You have to get to know Nick, because sometimes his remarks could be taken the wrong way.

He's grown up a lot the past three years. I believe that when Nick arrived, he was just trying to fit in. He was truly a kid. The Nick Collison I played with during my senior year was a man in every sense of the word. He was a strong presence on the floor, but more than that, he was a mature person.

Drew Gooden was always the one everybody knew would make it big. Drew arrived with a ton of talent, as athletic a person as I've ever played with on any team. He can be a goofy guy at times, doing things that seem downright silly. Drew can walk into the locker room

Clowning around with Drew Gooden.

singing a song and everyone will turn and look at him. He will tell jokes in a loud, exaggerated voice and break up the rest of the team. He was the California recruit, the guy with the social smarts who was coming to Kansas and believed he would immediately do things his way. It didn't quite work out like that.

Drew was extremely stubborn as a freshman. He had problems learning the system and was often at odds with the coaching staff. Drew could not understand why he was not allowed to do what he felt came naturally to him. He didn't appreciate the logic of fitting into a system that would eventually allow him to blossom as a basketball player.

There were times those early years when the relationship between Drew and Coach was on thin ice. He grew his hair out as a form of silent protest. There were a few times when Drew would not shave for days, just as we were about to play a game, something he did to send a signal to Coach Williams that he was not happy. On one occasion, we were playing a game against Iowa and Drew dressed and played in a pair of the early Jordans, some of the oldest and ugliest shoes he could have found. We all knew Coach was burning inside, but he never said anything to Drew in front of us.

Drew was not happy his first year. I know that he entertained thoughts of leaving Kansas, and he would talk about it at different times during the season.

Kirk Hinrich was the last of the three recruits that year. Kirk was the one regarded at the time as having the least talent, at least in the eyes of the press. Kirk was extremely quiet as a freshman, and it was an accomplishment if you could get him to say more than twelve words at any one time. To this day, I'd say that Kirk is the quietest guy on the team.

Kirk is a serious and competitive person. He often gets very mad at himself for mistakes he makes in practice. You have to remember that in his entire life, Kirk's only coach was his father. And there were times when he had a tendency to get mad when Coach Williams yelled at him in practice. Kirk would mutter to himself some reply and then get a determined look on his face. That's when anyone on the opposing team better watch out. It meant Kirk was going to take out his anger on the floor.

We were playing against Ohio State during Kirk's sophomore year, and he was playing defense. Somehow, the man he was guarding slashed Kirk above the eye as Kirk was trying to steal the ball. Kirk completed the steal and then, with his eye bleeding, he drove the length of the floor, wiping the blood from his eye. He made the shot at the other end and then called a timeout. Most guys would want the action stopped as soon as they were hurt. Not Hinrich. There was no way Kirk was going to call for help until he made that shot.

The other side of Kirk was visible when we took him to a party early in his freshman year. Some girls I knew were trying to get Kirk to open up. One of them began to dance with Kirk. I stood there, positive Hinrich would make a few moves and leave the floor. To my surprise, he began to bump and grind on the girl! Here was quiet, shy Kirk Hinrich becoming a whole new person when the music was on. I always tell people you have to spend a few months with Kirk before you really get to know him.

The new arrivals on this team were going to make an immediate impact. You could tell from the day they began to play with us, it seemed as if they had been there all along. The biggest competition and the burning question was whether Aaron Miles or Keith Langford would get the final starting spot. It seemed to me as though Aaron played the best at our early pickup games, but when practice began in mid-October, Keith seemed to shine. Suddenly, Aaron returned to his form of a few months earlier. It would be interesting to me to see which one Coach selected as a starter. I thought we'd benefit no matter which one he chose.

Those two guys and Wayne Simien, a huge freshman from Leavenworth, Kansas, were going to see a lot of playing time. At least, that's what I thought before the season began. They have the type of personalities that fill a locker room. As a freshman, I thought it best to remain kind of quiet and see how things went. Not these guys. They are full of laughter, like to talk loud and are a lot of fun. It's never dull or quiet when the freshmen arrive. I could tell they were going to have a good impact on this team. We would be loose and relaxed with them on board. That could prove to be an asset as the year went on.

We had four sets of roommates on this team. Kirk Hinrich roomed with Jeff Hawkins, Wayen Simien was with Keith Langford, Aaron Miles with his hometown friend Michael Lee and Drew

Gooden lived with Bryant Nash. Everyone else lived off campus, generally following my lead and living with non-basketball friends. Many guys like Nick Collison found friends from home had moved to Lawrence, just as my friends had done.

I wondered if this were unusual. Most people assume we all live together on the same floor of a dorm. If not a dorm, we have a special place on campus for jocks. It's not that way, and in fact, it is much different this year than any other time since I've been at KU. Coach wants us to be relaxed and focus on basketball when we take the floor each day for practice. Living this way helped this team be successful, I believe.

I know it did for me. I had been having problems my first two years, but now I was finding I enjoyed coming to Allen Fieldhouse more than my first two years. However, there was still the feeling that I was getting burned out. It just wasn't as much fun anymore. Basketball had been my life since I was five. I never thought I could feel this way, but I knew I needed a break from the game. One more season and I'd get that break. I was already planning what I would do when the year ended.

My plan was to take time off. Just get completely away from the game, if that were possible. I knew I would get a lot of calls from professional teams if I finished with a great senior season. And if we were to go far in the NCAA's, I'd really get the exposure needed to remind the scouts of my ability. This wasn't a bad thing.

However, I wanted to take at least a year off. I would finish my degree, relax and live like a normal student for a year. Sure I'd go to games and probably work out with the team every day. But I wouldn't have to think basketball, talk basketball or live basketball for 8 months. It would be great.

Then, when I had rejuvenated myself mentally, I'd make the attempt for the NBA. I'd go to the tryout camps and see if I had the ability. It would be better for me that way. I would be no good to anyone if I went straight from college to the pros. I was too burned out on the game for that.

This wasn't the best attitude to have as I entered my senior season, so I decided to keep this to myself. If I spent a lot of time with my friends at the apartment, I would have an easy time of ignoring the world of college ball. My roommates knew when to talk about basketball and when I was getting sick of hearing about it. Lon and Tim were living working lives and they had things to talk about as well. I became a good listener, and this lifestyle helped me tremendously.

The last part of my college career was about to begin. After three years of frustration, I was positive this was going to be the year. Even though I had been confident in my own ability as a sophomore, this team gave the impression that it was going to be the best on which I had ever played. That's why the start was so unexpected.

We were going to play in Hawaii. The Maui Invitational has to be one of the most unique places to begin a winter sport season. Everything I tend to associate with basketball is not present. The beach, the sun, the hot and humid gyms are not things I ever thought about when playing a winter sport. This was going to be our coming out party, the place where this Kansas team told the world we were the team to beat for the national title.

The last time a KU team was here, in 1997, they went on to run off 22 straight wins, be ranked number one most of the season, and compile numerous records both as individuals and as a team. They did not win the title, however, and the stigma of that season is something Kansas fans have never resolved. On one hand, it was a great time to be a fan, full of memorable games and athletes. On the other, it was such a heartbreaking ending. A lot of "what ifs?" remain.

The flight to Hawaii made me nervous. Not because of the games, but I hate flying for that length of time. We took a short flight to Dallas and then made the long, 8 hour flight to Maui. I was extremely glad to get off that plane, and being greeted by Hawaiian sunshine made it that much better. It seemed as though things would be great.

We practiced in some small, sweaty gym the first day. It was terrible, but probably a good thing, since we had a chance to get used to the warmth in conditions worse than any game. That night, every school was invited to a dinner opening the invitational. The food was great and it was a relaxed way to meet everyone from the other teams. EA Sports sponsored a PlayStation 2 tourney, where two guys from each school would play a team from another university on the new version of NBA Live. We were represented by Drew Gooden and Keith Langford, although Aaron Miles also got into the action. (I won't mention how they did, but Drew is better on the real floor!)

Good shooting form means fingertip control and proper rotation.

The next morning we played Ball State. An unusual part of this tourney is game time. We played games as early as 11 a.m., something we would never do for the rest of the season. Due to the TV committments and time differentials, games at the Maui Invitational are often played much earlier than those living on the mainland might think. It's not an excuse, but it was definitely something we never considered.

Ball State was a good team and our coaching staff had the team well prepared. I knew they would be hounding me all night, and realized I'd have to really work to get my shots. Nobody was expecting Ball State to shoot the record-setting way they did. It was one of those nights you hear about, where literally everything anyone threw up went in the basket.

At the half, we were in a state of shock. It's not like we didn't know what to do. We simply could not believe how well they were shooting. The coaching staff assured us that we could win this game if we kept out composure and played our game. That's what we tried to do the second half.

We made a good run at them, but Ball State continued their torrid shooting. It didn't seem as if we could find the right way to defend them, and some of those shots were the type that even the best defense could not prevent. I never got any solid looks at the basket all night and the heat gave Aaron Miles muscle cramps. Their defense was tough. They beat us 93-91.

The post-game locker room scene might surprise fans. The best word to describe Coach Williams was comforting. He reassured us about our ability as a team. He told us we ran into a good team on a hot night. And then he made a statement which seems almost eerie in retrospect. Coach Williams told us that the last time a Kansas team lost their opening game was 1993. That team made it to the Final 4.

We were on fire for the remainder of the tourney. Coach Williams handled us the right way and the team responded. We destroyed Houston and Seton Hall, two teams that simply could not keep up with the pace we were setting. It was as though we were determined to prove the first game wrong, to demonstrate to the critics that we were not a team that looked good only on paper. I had heard about comments from folks back home, that Coach was letting us fool around too much and not making us work seriously. Most of the

Using the shooting form I learned from my brother to hit a three-pointer against Missouri.

guys on the team were pretty mad at our fans back home when we read the comments about our vacationing instead of playing ball. Nothing was further from the truth.

It's hard at times to take this criticism. As a player, I know how hard my teammates and I work at practice. I see every day how all our coaches plan and work to make us a better team. I don't feel that any of the guys take their position lightly. In my mind, there wasn't one person on the Kansas team who slacked off in Hawaii, or for that matter, at any time during the season. We have pride in ourselves and we respect the coaches too much to do something like that.

After every game, the coaches go through a process of grading our performance. They will assemble and each member of the coaching staff is assigned something to record while watching the game tape. Each player is graded on various points of emphasis, from turnovers to assists to shot selection. We get our grades at the next days' practice.

As a team, we watch film on ourselves regularly. Coach Williams believes it's better for us to actually see how we are playing than for him to simply tell us. One aspect of his style is the fact that we rarely watch film of our opponents. We don't necessarily have to worry about stopping the team we are about to play. Coach believes that if we run our offense and defense correctly, it's the job of our opponents to stop us.

Now that I am removed from the program it's easier to see how fans could feel that we had too much fun in Hawaii and used that as a reason for our loss. I realize that some of our fans have seen too many disappointments to believe anything different. I guess this is one of those times where a person truly has to be there to understand that it was just not that way.

I receive a lot of fan mail asking about how I became a good shooter. Kids want some advice, parents want to know how their son or daughter can become a three point shooter. I wish I could give you set answer, but there isn't any one thing a person can do. I can offer my experiences as help, but that's about all.

I'd have to say there is one main thing to focus upon: long hours of work. I shot the ball sometimes as many as 6 hours a day those summers between 7th and 10th grade. I felt strange if I wasn't shooting, it became a part of my life, a daily routine that I had to continue. It's a form of addiction. That's not something you can tell someone to do. It's not something you were born with as a talent. You have to want to live your life this way. At that time in my life, I wanted to shoot a basketball as much as my arms and legs would allow.

By the time I was an 8th grader, I was frustrated with my shot. My shooting from beyond 15 feet was erratic. Sometimes I'd hit three straight, then miss 5 in a row, and often the shot would go to the left or right. Some guys might think this was due to my age and size. I felt I should be hitting the shots with more accuracy.

I went to my brother for help. Mike turned me into a jump shooter. He had me stand about 15 feet away from him and throw a chest pass. He caught it and threw it back. "Notice the rotation," Mike said. "It should be rotating front to back it should have back spin. Anytime the ball is moving side to side, your shot is going to be off in that direction." That advice has been burned into my brain. A good shooter will come up short or long if they miss. They will not be off to one side.

To get this down, I passed that ball with my brother for hours. I wasn't satisfied until nearly every pass I threw had back spin. We must have been up until 2 a.m., passing the ball. I'm not exaggerating about the time. I would not let someone leave until I was happy with what I was doing. Luckily, my brother cared enough to stand there for hours, watching and correcting me.

The next day I began to practice the shot, using the correct rotation. I started between 10 and 12 feet, shooting that jumper with the proper rotation. I'd never move beyond 15 feet. I was not going to take long shots until I was sure I could make the short ones the right way. If I had too many shots going to one side, I'd never leave that area until 80% of the shots started to go in with the proper rotation. That was the key. It wasn't good enough that they went in, they had to have that backspin.

I can be stubborn about things and in this case, that trait served me well. No doubt my friends were annoyed at times. Our summer workouts had to revolve around what I wanted to do when it came to shooting drills and now I was concentrating on the backspin. During AAU games that summer, I concentrated on getting shots no further than 15 feet from the hoop. I was not going to move further out until I could hit the close ones with accuracy and the proper spin. This meant the team had to set screens closer, defenses now thought I was becoming a decoy, but I didn't care. I was going to be an accurate shooter, and I was becoming successful.

Another asset people noticed is my quick release. Being 6'1" and playing against much taller opponents at the college level, it's difficult to get your shot off. I was lucky enough to be able to catch a pass and release my shot before some defenders could get to me. Sometimes I see myself on SportsCenter taking a shot which just makes it over some guy's fingertips. Unfortunately, there is nothing magical about this. It's also not something you can really work on developing. In my mind, it's a God-given ability. Either you can catch and release quickly, or you can't. It's like having good eyesight. You can't develop that into better eyesight. The same thinking applies to the quick release.

By the high school season, I had developed into a much better jump shooter. I started to move further out, getting into the 18 and 20 foot range. The process of becoming a long shot artist was slow. You don't just find it one morning. I worked for hours and was very determined as to how I wanted to progress. There is no magic to becoming an accurate shooter. It takes time and hard work.

Managers are the soul of the team. I know that may surprise some people, but I'm sure that it's true. It's a job I would never consider, yet I know how important they are to the success of the program.

We were leaving to fly home from Hawaii and I found myself watching as the managers were trying to keep track of everything. It dawned on me how much they do, how much I took for granted. I don't know if I would be able to worry or keep track of everything involved in moving our team from the rooms at the hotel to the airport.

Our managers do so much more than just hand out towels and keep the water bottles full. They assist in practice, keep statistics, make certain everything is ready for us when we arrive. It would be hard for me to think of doing this for basketball players, yet it's surprising how many managers were once basketball players themselves.

At first, one of the biggest adjustments I had to make at Kansas was having female managers. At Valley City, we were lucky to have a manager at all, but there was no way it would have been a female. She would have to put up with so much grief from the guys she would have quit. Either that or we would all have been in a lot of trouble.

The managers at Kansas are outstanding people. As players, we pack far less for road games than the managers. If we are playing a conference game, all I have to do is get my toiletries together, pack some underwear and be sure to bring a sport coat. Unless we are going to be staying longer than the normal post-game period, that's all I would need. We would arrive the night before the game, spend the next day getting ready for the game, play the game and get on the plane to go home.

The managers will pack everything we need. They have to pack all the equipment. They have to make sure everyone has the right uniform, shoes, socks and anything else that might be needed, whether it's for practice or for games. They are packing clothes for a dozen people, along with themselves. They are responsible for baggage check-in at any airports we might use, something that has been made much more difficult in today's world. After we get to the hotel, they have to make sure every bag is delivered to the correct room. When we get ready to leave the hotel, the whole process begins again. Starting with the players rooms, the managers have to get everything ready for when we leave that hotel.

It's a fact of our lives that once the season ends, we probably take three to four weeks to adjust to doing all of our laundry again. The managers wash our practice gear, and that includes everything down to the socks. I became spoiled in this regard. I knew that towels would always be there and be clean. I knew that my practice jerseys and shorts would be ready for me to pick up and put on every day. If this sounds as though I was lazy about some of these things, I admit I was. During my first two years at Kansas, there were times when I would shrug and think to myself that it's their job. They're the managers.

One of my friends at Kansas is Jeff Hackel. He's from a small town in Nebraska and as a manager, he does so many different things. The guys tease Jeff and tell him he is the personal slave for one of the female managers. He handles the friendly abuse well, smiling and joking in return. Jeff has an easygoing personality and is a lot of fun. We have worked together the past two summers cleaning swimming pools and I've gotten to know him away from basketball. It takes a special type of person to handle this job, and he's one of the few I know who can do it and enjoy their work. Managers have to be able to adjust to our different moods, and that's not always easy.

I guess it's the same in any sport. The guys who play the game sometimes take things for granted, and having managers performing the little tasks is not always noticed or appreciated. I felt the managers have never gotten the true measure of respect they deserve. They get paid by the month, but it's not a tremendous amount of money, certainly not when you consider the work they perform. Getting to know Jeff made me think about this a little more. He never complains, he's always got a smile on his face and yet the job he has to do is never recognized publicly. When I took the time to consider these things, it made me realize how lucky all of us on the team are to have these people around.

It's only been four years since I finished high school. Yet, some things about basketball have changed dramatically. I'd have to say that one of the most controversial is the growth of AAU summer basketball. The evolution of this aspect of the game surprises me. AAU ball helped me get to where I am today. Yet, there are some things I see that bother me.

I will never say AAU basketball is better than high school basketball. It's an entirely different program. High school basketball is as traditional as you can get. The Friday night game, the crowds of friends, family and classmates, the cheerleaders and everything that goes with school sports is part of growing up in America. Part of any high school is attending or talking about the games, whatever the sport. We have built an entire subculture around this.

Yet, sometimes I look at high school ball and feel sad. In the minds of the top players, AAU is now the way to go, and the idea of playing for the town or school seems to be losing appeal. It's part of what I see as a more selfish society, and unfortunately it's creeping into high schools more and more.

The reasons are varied. Top players want to be seen by as many colleges as possible. I was the same way. I wanted to be seen by Kansas. The reality is that many colleges do not search the nation for talent. They go to the areas where they feel they will be able to see many talented players in a short period of time. Being from North Dakota, this meant I would never be seen. Our towns are small, there are less schools and thus less athletes. The perception is that we are not able to compete at the top level because we don't face top level competition. While I feel this is not always true, and that my home state has many good athletes, it is a fact that I didn't face as many tough opponents in high school as someone who played in the Los Angeles area.

Players like AAU ball because you go to a gym and play possibly 10 games in 3 days. If you have a bad game, you only have to wait a few hours to play again and change things around. In high school, the next game is likely to be a week later. Poor performances eat away at your confidence. Consider the coach who is in town recruiting. At the high school game, he sees a bad night and leaves, and may never be able to return. In the AAU format, the bad game would be followed by a good game two hours later. The coach is in town for the entire day. He will be able to see you play three times. It gives the player a chance to make up for a bad outing and impress the scout, not only with a better game, but also with the demonstration of how you can bounce back from adversity.

Since AAU teams can pick and choose who they want to participate, it allows coaches to assemble the equivalent of a college team. A coach can select 8 top players and not worry about things like playing everyone equal amounts of time, grade eligibility, disciplinary action, and other school related problems. In high schools, you have to pick your team from the athletes who live in town or attend the school. If you are a great player, surrounded by many average athletes, you may not look as good and thus will never get the chance to show what you could do on a better team. The top players in high schools today tend to think they are better off on a team with other superior athletes. They lean towards the AAU programs.

Coaches are undermined by this. The dilemma for the high school coach is obvious. In the summer, the players are often told they are free to do what they do best. AAU teams tend to be loosely structured on offense, with only basic plays for both offense and defense. This freedom allows guys to demonstrate their ability without throwing off a game plan or set offense. High school coaches tend to try and develop a true team atmosphere. This means running things that are best for a team victory but not necessarily best for an individual to shine.

Some college coaches now talk to the AAU coach before they get in contact with the high school coach. To me, this encourages the players to go AAU and gives that team an aura of importance more

so than the high school. After all, if the AAU coach is the one the college calls to talk about you, wouldn't you listen to that guy over your high school coach?

There is nothing wrong with what high schools are doing. Valley City High School had great team when I played there. Our coaches were good men who taught me well. Kansas is a program that stresses virtually everything I have mentioned in regards to high schools. Coach Williams does not let us run wild, get poor grades and try and do things to impress NBA scouts so that individuals can get pro contracts. We do things with a team philosophy, and work together for the betterment of everyone. It succeeds and I completely believe in what we do at KU.

However, most guys know AAU or the Nike and Adidas camps are the only way you will get to the NCAA Division I level of athletics. Shane Power, a starter from Iowa State, once told me that after attending the Adidas camp in New Jersey, he knew those 200 guys were going to be the guys he competed against the next four years. They were treated better than he had ever seen in any team camp or at any high school event. It was obvious, especially from the speakers who talked to the guys during that week, these athletes were above other high schoolers. They were regarded as a special class of basketball player. It seemed to Shane that no matter how well anyone did in high school, if a guy were not invited to one of these camps, he should give up any hopes of playing for a top 25 Division I program.

The only exception to this I have ever known is Marlon London, my first roommate at Kansas. Marlon never played AAU basketball. He never attended the Nike or Adidas camps. He didn't travel all over the nation with a team in the summer. He simply played for his high school, and it was not a state championship team. They had a season record that was slightly above average. Yet Marlon happened to get noticed by college scouts and eventually Coach Williams heard about him and recruited him to KU. This method of making it to Division I can still occur, but it is becoming a rarity.

"What's best for me" seems to be what I hear many kids say, and their parents are in agreement. It's sad and I don't think it's right. I liked playing AAU basketball. It gave me a chance I might not have received had I only played for Valley City High. Yet, I would never have traded away the chance to play for the Hi-Liners. Playing for my hometown was more appealing than just playing for some guy who put together a team for the summer. To this day I will tell people I played for Valley City. I don't know the last time I told anyone what the names of the various AAU teams were. I don't even know if I could remember....

Chapter 6

December

GOING HOME

December has been a very good month for Kansas basketball for quite some time. I can't give you a specific reason why, but we always seem to play well before Christmas. It's not like we have a cupcake schedule. Our non-conference opponents generally contain at least 5 teams who will have been ranked at the time we play them. We play many of these opponents on the road. Yet, we rarely lose these games.

I've tried to think about why this happens. From my own perspective I know I'm always very anxious to play real games rather than continued practice. It's possible this makes us more focused on basketball, on doing what the coaches want and just full of desire to get out there and pound someone other than teammates.

Maybe it's the end of the semester as well. Final exams come early in December, generally the second week. It's true that athletes who have their time budgeted for practice, study and relaxation in a tight manner can become more productive in all three areas. We have such a tight schedule during the first 6 weeks of the season that there is little time for us to get relaxed. We emerge as angry warriors, a team you would not want to play and certainly not take lightly.

This year we traveled to Arizona and defeated them on their home floor. We played Wake Forest and Tulsa as well, and defeated them as well, scoring in the 90's in both games. We were really clicking on offense, and much of that success was actually due to our defense, something many people overlooked.

Our offense is so varied it throws opponents off their game. One of the distinguishing features about a Kansas team is the nature of the scoring. It never comes from one person. We may have someone who is quite an offensive threat, but we never rely solely on that individual. We have a balanced scoring attack, and it's one of the main reasons we are hard to beat.

My game is a perfect example. Occasionally I receive letters from fans who tell me to shoot more often. These are generally from young ballplayers who see me as an accurate long range shooter. "Why," they wonder, "don't you shoot the ball more? You could score 25 points every game. Does Coach Williams tell you not to shoot?"

It never hurts to let your teammates know you need help on defense.

The reason I don't shoot more often is I don't want to. Being a guard in either the one or two position means you are in charge of the offense. My job is to make certain the team takes the best shot it can get. I'm not always in that position. Simply because the ball is in my hands as we come up the floor doesn't mean I look to shoot the ball. I try to see if someone else is in a better position to take a shot.

Teams also consider things such as the foul situation of our opponents. I might have an open look from 22 feet and it might be a shot I know I can easily hit. But if the man guarding Nick has three fouls, and I see the chance, I'll get the ball inside to Nick. I'm hoping he can draw a foul out of his defender, forcing the coach to take that man out of the game. It might cost me a few chances to score, but for our team's success, this is the way I'd always play it.

Younger players have to remember that there will always be a chance to score. It's not important how many shots any one individual takes during a game. What's important is whether or not your team wins. Being on a successful team is much more enjoyable than losing most of your games. College coaches don't look only at the top scorers as potential recruits. An important point to remember is that coaches want to see how you as a player helped your team win games. Being on a winning team might get you noticed more than having a scoring average of 26 points a game on a team that loses 14 games out of 20 in a high school season.

If you are an accurate shooter, you don't have to worry. You'll get your shots and they will fall. Work on your game, improve your shot and things will be fine. In the meantime, for those who wonder why I don't take so many shots in a game, I point to our record. How many games has Kansas lost over the past three years?

Every year, Coach Williams tries to make certain that seniors from out of state get to play a game in their home state. This year, it was my turn. And on December 23, I returned to North Dakota, to play my first and only college basketball game in my home state.

The folks from North Dakota made this a night I would always remember. As game time approached, the lights were dimmed. A highlight film of my Kansas career was shown. I don't know who assembled this, but I was stunned and could feel goosebumps all over my body as I watched myself on the giant screen.

Waving to the fans, both KU and North Dakota.

When the tribute film was over, the 14,000 people in the arena stood and cheered. The ovation lasted nearly a minute, and I became very emotional. It was something I'd never experienced and it made me realize how lucky I was. The people of my home state were letting me know that I would always be one of them, no matter where I went. It was a very nice gesture on their part and it made me think about how I had changed in the three years since I had left home.

I think being raised in a state the size of North Dakota makes a person look for the good in other people. That's a decent trait. It allows people to be more positive in their dealings with others. Look at our newspapers for an example of this. When stories are written about citizens in the state or about athletes, they tend to focus on something good the individual has done. If a game is lost, then it's lost. If a promise is not kept, it's a broken promise. The facts are stated clearly and in a straightforward manner. There is not an attempt to analyze the character of that person or imply some questionable motive. I think that's the negative approach too many newspapers found in larger cities and states try to take. It's harmful to the people involved and, in my opinion, it means you are looking for the worst in people, rather than expecting the best from them.

I feel I'm an honest person and I tend to trust other people implicitly. I've noticed, however, that after a few years of being in the spotlight and dealing with the press, I've become more cautious around strangers. I don't assume anymore that someone will be as honest with me as I am with them. What bothers me is that I don't like the person I've had to become. There are days when I wish I could be as open as I used to be when I lived in North Dakota.

It may sound naive, but I know my home town, and this is a true statement: growing up in Valley City was easier and better than many other places I know or have heard about. Sure, we had our problems, but nothing on the scale of what my teammates and KU acquaintances have told me about their hometowns. There were kids who drank to excess and smoked pot. People I've met from places like Chicago, Dallas or St. Louis had as many as one-third of their classmates doing coke or acid. I never heard of anyone selling those drugs at our high school, and the only people who seemed to be talking about it a lot were the college kids who came back from out of state.

We aren't saints nor are we perfect. But I truly believe people from North Dakota are more decent, positive and honest than those from most other places in this country. I'm lucky because after living here the past few years, I realize that Kansas may be the closest to my home state in many of these respects. The people I've met from small towns like Emporia, Lindsborg or Horton seem to be the most like the folks back home.

My brother Mike was also honored, along with the other members of the University of North Dakota basketball team from 1989-90. They made it to the Elite Eight in the NCAA Division 2 tourney that year, the best showing ever for a North Dakota basketball team. To make the night complete, it was the first time my grandmother ever saw me play in college. The location for this game, Englestad Arena, is actually an ice arena used by the University of

North Dakota. All 14,000 seats are covered with leather, the floors are made of marble and every seat has an unobstructed view. It's quite an impressive place.

The game was one of the best of my career. The previous year, North Dakota had really shut me down, playing a very tight defense on me all night. This time it was different. I was determined to play well, and it seemed as if my cuts were sharper coming off screens. It was one of those nights when everything seemed to fall my way, and I ended the night with 23 points. We won the game handily.

The team showered and dressed quickly, since the weather was starting to get bad. I knew everyone wanted to get out and on the road, but I couldn't get myself moving. I was staying here with my family and saw no need to rush. The events of the night were still playing through my mind. I was thinking about the ceremony, and about life in North Dakota.

I was coming out of this daydream when I heard someone run into the locker room. "Jeff?," a voice called out. It was Coach Williams. I was standing in a far corner of the locker room and looked at Coach. As we made eye contact, he said, "Merry Christmas." In that moment, I felt closer to him than I had during my four years at Kansas. It was typical of Coach to do something like this, to run back and make sure I didn't feel forgotten as the rest of the team was leaving.

"Merry Christmas, Coach," I replied. "And thanks."

The coaching staff learned the team could not fly out of Grand Forks due to the snow and high wind gusts. To make matters worse, the Minneapolis airport was about to close due to the snow. Coach Williams had decided to let those players who had family at the game drive home. Nick and Kirk went home to Iowa with their parents. Jeff Carey drove back to Missouri with his folks. Obviously, I stayed in Valley City.

One of the fears everyone had expressed about playing a game in North Dakota near Christmas was snow. The guys had made a lot of jokes about getting stranded in the middle of nowhere. Considering the normal weather pattern for December, it was a very real possibility. And that's exactly what happened.

The team left the arena and snow was building in intensity. The guys were getting worried about being stranded. The coaching staff talked things over and decided the best thing to do was to get a bus and drive back to Kansas City. Although it was one of the nice cruiser style buses, it was still going to be a very long trip.

Drew was especially irritated about this. He is not the type to sit still for that long, and a bus no matter how nice, is still a bit cramped for guys who are nearly 7 feet tall. To make matters worse, since the team had not planned to travel this way, there were no movies for anyone to watch. Due to the time they left, there were no places to eat which were open. The guys were not happy and of course, someone mentioned whose fault this was.

"You know, Bosch's sittin' somewhere all nice and cozy right now," Brett Ballard said to one of the managers.

"Yeah, we'll have to make sure we thank him for all of this," Jeff Hackel replied, in a sarcastic tone.

"Maybe I'll forget to give him a clean towel for a few days."

By the time they arrived in Lawrence, the Kansas Jayhawks had been on the road for nearly 15 hours, most of it driving slowly through snow covered roads with a howling wind outside. For guys who are used to traveling on planes, it was quite a change. The team did stop in Watertown, S.D., to stretch their legs, do some essential shopping and get something to eat. Some of the guys bought a few videos to watch on the bus as they continued the long, slow trip back home.

Because they arrived on campus the day before Christmas, they were not happy. And of course, someone mentioned (quite a few times) that this was all my fault for being born in a state like North Dakota. Had the guys seen me they might have been more upset. While they were sitting cramped in that bus, I was at home enjoying the holidays.

Without a doubt, my favorite time of year is Christmas. I guess I am just one of those people who likes things the old fashioned way around the holidays. I'll play the music for a month and never get tired of it. This is the one time of year I want snow, and usually lots of it. I cannot imagine how to enjoy Christmas without snow. Valley City has got to be one of the best locations anyone could spend Christmas. It fits every stereotype about the holiday season, from the tree branches covered with snow to the way everyone decorates their homes. Movies could not be made to look as real as my hometown during the holidays.

Bozo spent my senior year in Valley City. My mom became attached to him, and he seemed to take to the new surroundings. What's cool about a dog is how they recall you, even after being separated for months. When I walked into my home after the game, Bozo went crazy. He jumped all over me, licking and barking, acting as if I was the greatest present he could get for Christmas. It's hard not to smile when he's acting that way. The dog was really giving me a Christmas greeting.

Our family does the same thing every year for the holidays, and that's another thing I like. This is one day I believe should keep a traditional approach, and to me that means not changing things very much year to year. We do much of the celebrating on Christmas Eve, with Mom cooking everyone's favorite meal. This means I get lasagna, my brother gets what he wants, so does my father and my mother makes something for herself. If any relatives are over, they also get what they want. We are up late that night.

Christmas Day after church means turkey. My mother does it up right, with all the trimmings you'd expect. If this sounds like a lot of work for her, it is. Yet she enjoys doing this, and it's part of what I associate with Christmas. If I never said this before I should have. I love you Mom for making this such a special day.

Chapter 7

January

NEW YEAR'S SURPRISE

The team was playing good ball as the new year began. We were racking up some impressive statistics, becoming the highest scoring team in the nation. Our record reached 12-1 and by January 6th we finally reached the top. We were ranked number one in the polls. We played at Nebraska three days later and crushed them, 96-57. It felt great to be number one.

The excitement surrounding us was starting to mount. Fans who had doubted us were being won over by our style of play. The mail I was receiving was growing in volume. Some days, it was ridiculous how much mail was coming in my name to the basketball office. Every guy on the team was getting more mail than ever, which was something we talked about in the locker room.

None of us seemed to have the time to reply to the letters which were pouring in. It was easier to respond to e-mailed fan letters, but even those were clogging up our mailboxes. Many of these e-mails were very personal and often dealt with one question or issue. It's as though the people who wrote those letters wanted to include the players in their personal arguments.

I was getting mail which asked me if I thought Kirk or Brett were the better guard. Some letters would ask if Brett was dating someone or if Keith had a girl back home. Most were asking if I were going with someone or if I could meet them after the next game.

Occasionally, questions would revolve around a specific part of the last game, and the sender would want to know why I took a particular shot or why I passed up what they perceived as an opportunity to score. It was fun at first, but after a while these letters became monotonous. It was almost a relief to hit the road for the next game.

We headed west for a big game against UCLA. It was the CBS game of the week, one of the first of the college basketball season. The Bruins were ranked in the top ten, and we were playing our first game as top dog. It was the first time I had ever played for a team who was ranked number one. I'd always thought it would be so cool to be on a top ranked team. When I was younger, it was one of those dream things. Now that it was real, the odd thing was there didn't seem to be any more pressure than any other game.

The day before the game was our day to experience Los Angeles. Coach arranged for us to attend the premier of a movie in Hollywood. We were taken to a location and watched as many celebrities did exactly what you see if you are watching "Entertainment Tonight." People got out of limousines and walked the length of a red carpet to the entrance, waving at the crowd as they entered. I'm not that into celebrity watching, but I did recognize Frankie Muniz from the TV show "Malcolm in the Middle." Chris Zerbe captured the entire scene on his video camera, and he was trying to sneak himself in to a better position by pretending to be a real photographer.

As we were leaving, Aaron Miles kept saying that the rapper Ludacris was actually in the crowd, trying to be with the real people. Drew, who could see over everyone, kept looking and finally saw Ludacris. He was surrounded by his bodyguards, so I don't think he was really trying to associate with the average fan. We went to the California Pizza Kitchen afterwards, for some West Coast food. As always, there was a 11 p.m. team meeting before we went to our rooms for the night. Coach does this to make sure we realize the emphasis of the trip now is changing. Having a scouting session helps us focus back onto the game we'll play the next afternoon.

Kansas was supposed to be playing UCLA, but an entirely different team showed up. We made so many bad passes, we took so many bad shots and were so sluggish getting back on defense, it didn't seem real. I can't explain why or how this happened. None of us can. The entire team seemed to be there physically but not mentally. We made a run at them late in the game, and the final score would be misleading as to how close a contest it was. It's a game I never wanted to watch again, and one that I tried to put out of my mind as soon as it ended. UCLA kicked our butts that afternoon.

Afterwards, we were apprehensive going into the locker room. Everyone knew how badly we had performed. Even Nick couldn't think of a thing to say that would shake the mood. We assembled in our usual spots, ready to take whatever Coach had to say.

We were in for a surprise. Coach Williams never exploded. He calmly told us that we should now realize how we had to play if we were really the top ranked team in America. He reassured us of his faith in our ability and simply told us this was nothing more than a bump in the road. It was exactly what we needed to hear.

I believe this team was the most mature group of guys I've ever been associated with, in a basketball sense. We knew in our minds how to win, but not in our hearts. At that point in the season, we were not ready to play in the big game. The UCLA game showed us we had to learn how to play a determined game, with poise and heart. We had been running away from our opponents, beating them with a fast paced game. Much of the reason for this was our talent level, knowledge and desire had been superior. We were one of the best teams out there.

To be the BEST team, we had to climb up to a higher level. There were a few teams out there who could match us in ability. That meant we had to become a different team, a better team than we were in early January. After this game, the guys came to realize what we needed to do.

I hate to lose. There is an old saying that I've always felt was strange. It the one that says sometimes there is such a thing as a good loss. For this game, it was probably a true statement. It was a good loss for us to endure because we learned from it. The rest of the season would prove that.

We were out for dinner at Chipotle's, a Mexican place in downtown Lawrence. The dining room is open, and people walk through to get their carry out orders. I was sitting with Lon and Tim, talking and not paying attention to anyone in particular. As I was about to take a bite from one of the giant burritos, a voice from behind said, "Hey Jeff, can I get you to sign this?" Not recognizing the voice, I turned around and looked at a man who was wearing a KU shirt and jeans. I had never seen him before in my life. Not wanting to be rude, I said, "Sure, let me see what you've got there." I took the jersey, signed my name, and returned the jersey and pen to the guy. I thought I would get a chance to continue my dinner. Instead, he began a conversation about the basketball team.

Some people feel this is a trade off we make. It has been pointed out that basketball players get full scholarships plus free room and board. We get to travel and represent Kansas throughout the United States. We stay in great hotels, eat well and meet some prominent people. Our pictures are in newspapers and magazines, we get interviewed for television and radio programs and posters of us are sold to kids all across America. We get the fame and recognition; in return we give up our privacy.

I don't feel that way. Nobody has the right to someone's personal life. At the game, after the game, autographs are fine. I enjoy doing them, especially for kids. The look in a kids' eye when he makes contact with me, when I shake his or her hand and talk for a minute, is priceless. It's one of the things I'm going to miss the most about not playing for Kansas. Anytime a young person wants something, I'm glad to do it.

Adults are another story. The calls at home and the interruptions of a conversation when I'm with friends are actions I consider borderline rude. A lot depends on the manner of the person. If you were to see me and say, "Excuse me Jeff, I'd like to ask you something" I probably would turn to you and listen. What amazes me is how some people just walk up and start talking, even if I'm in the middle of another conversation. If their own children did that to them, I have no doubt those people would reprimand their child. Yet they see nothing wrong with doing it to me.

I know it's a part of being a KU ballplayer and some of the guys just eat that stuff up. I don't. I've always been a private person, and I guess that's been one of the hardest adjustments I had to make while being a college basketball player. I was brought up to respect another person's privacy.

I've gotten a lot of phone calls throughout my career at home, and they aren't all from women. For that matter, I wouldn't say they were from fans. People will call me at home and start to trash talk about my ability, they will make comments about the last game or the next game, and the whole thing amazes me. Lon and Tim, my roommates, just shake their heads in wonder. I keep coming back to the same thought. Why would anyone want to take time out of their day to call and harass me? Since I have never met these people, what is it that makes them want to call me and try to get me ticked off?

Some of the calls are from high school kids, and those I can almost understand. After all, they live right in town, probably see us numerous times, and might even be basketball players themselves. I can picture them sitting around their rooms, 3 or 4 guys laughing while the caller is insulting me. It makes them feel as if they got away with something. At that age, it's easier to see why it's done.

But grown men? People who probably have families and kids of their own? When they call and talk to me about why I suck, why Kansas is overrated, or how we're going to lose our next game, I am completely baffled. Are they at work when they're making these calls? What's the point?

Most of our home games have the same ending. The horn sounds and we run off the court. The team goes into the locker room and celebrates for a few minutes, getting all the energy and adrenaline out of our system. The length of this depends on the opponent. I won't lie about this, if the team we were playing is somebody I felt we were supposed to beat, I don't get as excited. There are some teams I knew we should beat, due to our talent level and experience. I couldn't get as thrilled after those wins. But if we had a tougher game than expected, or if it was someone I thought was going to be a real challenge, I'd be as crazy as everyone else in that room.

Most of the guys were the same as me. Games like Arizona and Missouri were followed by lengthy celebrations. It took a while for us to settle down. There were other games, like the first Kansas State game this year, when it was almost a matter of fact approach. It's hard to explain why, it's just a mood that comes over me, and some of the other guys as well.

We will eventually all take our seats in front of our lockers. Coach Williams gives us his initial thoughts about the game. Next, a couple of the guys will move to the media area to answer questions from the press. The selected players might be predetermined, but often are requested by the reporters present after the game. Sometimes there might be a little food for us, brought in by the managers. This might occur after a late Monday night game. By the time this is all done, we can shower and leave.

Fans line the hallways surrounding our locker room exits. This is something I looked forward to after every home game. The KU faithful, waiting for autographs or a chance to take a picture with one of us. The hallways are full in every direction. I remember after the Missouri game, I came out and found what looked like a larger than normal crowd. After what seemed to be a half hour of signing, the crowd didn't appear to have become any smaller.

"Hey Nick," I asked Collison, who was standing next to me in the roped off area, "is this crowd getting any smaller?"

"I don't know, Bosch," Nick said in reply.

"Well, look out there," I said.

"I can't see that far," Collison deadpanned.

I turned to give him a look. He's 6'10" and could easily see over anything in the Fieldhouse. I glanced at Nick's face and saw a wicked grin starting to form. He was going to have fun with me. He leaned over and whispered,

"Bosch, if you want to see out there, just jump up and give these women a thrill. They'll all think you are trying to find one of them." He moved away a few feet and said something to Kirk.

Kirk moved over closer to where I was standing. As he did, he started to get a smile on his face. He kept on signing a poster and didn't even look at me as he spoke.

"Want me to lift you up so you can see?" he asked with a short laugh. Then Kirk threw in the clincher.

"Girls," Hinrich called out to the crowd, raising his voice a bit, "Jeff Boschee wants to be able to see all of you. Could the shorter girls move to the front?"

There was a sudden increase in the volume of talking, as the higher pitch of female voices took over the noise level of the crowd. A large throng of girls moved to where I was standing. Kirk and Nick moved away, smiling proudly at their accomplishment. I was now surrounded and had no choice but to keep on signing. I could feel my eyes widen helplessly as I looked at them with the grins on their faces.

"Damn Iowa boys," I said to myself, smiling and knowing they had gotten me.

Eventually the crowd thinned out and I realized I was the only guy left signing things. The game had ended two hours earlier. It didn't seem that long ago.

Ticket requests are a fact of life when you play for a program like ours. The seating capacity of Allen Fieldhouse is 16,300, and there are never any spare tickets to be found. It may surprise you to find out that the players are limited to 4 tickets per home game. Those tickets include parents. When it comes to special situations, such as the NCAA tournament, each guy on the team gets 6 tickets. That's it.

This makes it tricky when trying to fill those requests from friends who want to come and see Kansas play. My parents tried to make it to most of the home games. If both of my roommates came to a game, that would use up my allotment for that night. Obviously, there is a lot of trading, or borrowing of tickets among teammates. Guys with large families really have to scramble to try and accommodate everyone. Inevitably, there are going to be nights when some relative or close friend is going to have to be told they can't get in.

People assume we can just get as many seats as we want. I guess it's a logical thing to believe but it's simply not the case. We play the games, but we have absolutely no control over the tickets we can get. Actually, I like it this way because it relieves me of the problem of trying to get a large number of tickets for people. Of course I want my friends to come and see me play, but I don't like the hassle of being a ticket manager.

The crowds line up outside Allen Fieldhouse to get tickets for a home game.

My roommate Tim has a great attitude about this. He once told me "I've seen you play since high school. I'm not that crazy about waiting in long lines to get inside the Fieldhouse on a cold night. I don't really enjoy being crammed into a bleacher seat. And I can get a better view of the whole game on television. So don't worry about me when it comes to tickets. If you've got one left, I'll take it, but otherwise give it to someone else."

To the campers who wait inside Allen Fieldhouse, keeping a spot in the line to buy tickets, this is unheard of. These fans/students will wait for as long as a week to buy these coveted seats. They will form groups of people who take turns sitting in a spot, holding it until they can buy those tickets. It's as bad as any rock concert, and consider that this is in winter. Even though they are inside, this is an old fieldhouse, and it's drafty. The floor is cement, and there aren't that many facilities.

Occasionally Coach Williams has bought donuts for these students. I know that people bring in food for them to eat. Someone is designated to have the overnight shift, which means sleeping on the floor. It's quite a scene and it takes place all season long. The better we play, the longer the wait for tickets. Our fans are amazing. If they knew that Tim would give up his potential seat so easily, they'd be all over him in a heartbeat.

Believe it or not, there are also students who could care less about the basketball team. This really should not come as a surprise. Not everyone is a fan of basketball. And at Kansas, there are many students who resent the publicity we receive. Whether they are in another sport, a fraternity or just are not into any sports, these people don't like us because we are on the basketball team.

Right after my junior season ended, some of the guys went to a bar in Lawrence. We wanted to mingle with other students, relax and have a good time. We were standing there, deciding if we wanted to get something, walk around for a few minutes, or leave and head somewhere else. Right then, a guy pushed his way past me, stood at the bar and ordered a drink. He then looked at me and said "Sorry, were you ordering something?" "No," I replied, "go ahead and get what you want." As the guy turned and picked up his drink, I heard the bartender tell him, "Don't worry about that dude. I wouldn't serve him before you anyway. He's a basketball player and I don't like any of those guys."

If there is one thing I've noticed, it's that the fame people associate with us doesn't translate into special treatment from everyone we meet. Sometimes it's understandable. For example, three or four of the basketball players will walk into a bar or Applebee's type place. Immediately, a group of girls will flock to our side. They all start talking at once, laughing and making us feel pretty darn special. For us, it's a great experience. For the guys they were with, it's a reason to get mad.

This past spring, the senior KU basketball players went on a barnstorming trip around the state, staging games against local coaches, teachers and athletes. We were playing a game in Hays, a town in western Kansas, and the event was late in the afternoon. Afterwards, we decided to go somewhere in town and get something to eat. Brett Ballard was standing outside a diner, waiting for Jeff Carey and I to arrive. A guy about our age starts looking at Brett, walks over and gets right in his face. He kept up the stare and finally Brett said, "See anything you like?" The guy backed off a step, kept up the glare and said, "You know, I'm a wrestler and I hate all you basketball fags. I think I'll kick your ass right here." Jeff and I came walking up, just in time to hear this. We all looked at the guy and went inside. I wondered if he were going to try anything when we left, but he wasn't around.

Afterward I received a letter from a fraternity member who had heard about the incident. This surprised me because we were in town for a total of about 4 hours. Yet this person wrote to me and apologized on behalf of others, saying that although this wrestler was a jerk, many people in Hays supported KU basketball. It was a nice gesture on his part, but not necessary. I realize that our fame can be double-edged, and that some people feel we get too much for contributing too little.

This brings me to another point. There are stories about how college athletes should be happy with the scholarships they receive. Others feel we should be paid for playing, since we don't have a chance to get jobs that would allow us to have spending money. The time we could be spending working is time we are using to become better players. This is an issue discussed on sports talk shows whenever there is a slow news day.

My feeling is that I received a scholarship as a reward for being a good player. All the work I did when I was young allowed me to reach a level of ability that others couldn't match. To demonstrate how this was appreciated, Kansas is paying for my education. In return, I promise to play to the best of my ability and to reflect positively on the university and the state of Kansas.

Sports is a business. College sports is in a gray area. Huge sums of money are spent on equipping a team, traveling around the nation, educating and feeding us and making sure we are healthy. That money comes from the sale of tickets and television rights. Because we are a successful program, we generate much interest and can create a lot of revenue for the university. Yet the people who are actually bringing in the money receive no physical cash.

I don't know the answer. I know that students who don't like athletes will comment that they cannot get much in the way of financial aid, yet we get full rides. They would have to get much higher grades to get even one fifth of what we receive, no matter our academic performance. Some resent this. I can only state my opinion. We bring in recognition and money to KU. We don't get paid. The scholarship is our pay. Some people earn their way to college by working two or three jobs, or by studying hours and hours to achieve excellent grades. I worked hours and hours to become a better 3-point shooter. We did the same thing, just in different areas. We all worked hard to get what we wanted.

The little boy couldn't have been more than 8 years old. He was wearing a jersey that had my name on the back with the number 13. When he turned around, I saw it was Kansas jersey with my number displayed on the front. The boys eyes lit up as I ran in front of him on my way to the court. It was obvious to me that I was the person he held in his mind as his favorite player.

The idea that I could be someone's favorite basketball player is still something I can't comprehend. Getting letters in the mail telling me how much my style of play means to someone makes me look at my life differently. There is nothing anyone can say to prepare you for how it will feel to know others want to be like you. Maybe the word is awesome.

Certainly there is a feeling of responsibility I would not have felt as a freshman. Fresh out of high school, I don't think I understood how important it is to act in a manner that reflects positively upon everyone ever associated with you. My actions tell the world what kind of parents I have, how their values are demonstrated through me. Sometimes kids think they can do what they want. I know I used to say, "who cares what other people think?" Seeing the jerseys in stores, having my picture on posters I know will be hanging on someone's bedroom wall and getting e-mails have changed my attitude.

We are only college basketball players to most people but to the kids we are more. We represent something they can aspire to become. In my own case, part of the appeal could be my physical stature. I'm not someone who had the good fortune to grow to a large height. Often young basketball players think they will not succeed because they are average in stature. If anyone were to look at me, they might not even realize I play college basketball. I'm not known for breakaway dunks and I am not blessed with blazing speed. If I were to move into a crowd of 100 people, and those people were not Kansas fans, it's possible nobody would pick me as the Division I athlete.

I think that's important for anyone to remember. There is a way to make your dreams come true, but it doesn't appeal to everyone. It's called dedication. You must be dedicated to your goals and believe in yourself. I know how this sounds, and it's been told to people for generations. That doesn't mean it isn't true. I hope that every kid who is wearing my jersey or looking at my poster realizes they can be the next guy to be in my spot. If they get there, they'll understand what I mean.

Jonas Sahratian, the strength coach, has to stretch us out before games. Although we are in our prime physical years, we have to follow a regimen designed to get the peak performance from us every game. Brett Ballard and I were roommates on the road and Jonas came up to our room.

"Alright guys, who's first?" he asked

"I might as well get you excited first, Jonas," I said. "Get your hands ready for some fun!"

"Shut up, Boschee, and lay on your stomach," he said.

Just as Jonas started the butterfly stretch, I farted. It was unintentional, but it was loud. I started laughing uncontrollably, and Brett was in hysterics.

"Damn you Jeff," Jonas said, "quit fooling around and let me stretch you out. You're not the only guy on the team who needs stretching."

"Okay," I said. Just as he was leaning forward, I farted again. Another loud one, right near his face.

"That's it!" he shouted. "I'm taking Ballard first and you can just go sit on the can and get rid of whatever is making your butt act up."

I tried to apologize, but it's hard to be taken seriously when you are laughing as much as I was. Whatever I had at lunch was taking its toll.

Brett stretched himself out on his stomach and spread his legs to begin the butterfly. I was sitting in an easy chair, watching and trying to compose myself. Jonas began working on his legs, and was at it for about one minute when Brett farted. It was about as loud as mine had been and I laughed so hard I fell off the chair. Brett was now hysterical with laughter and it was obvious Jonas was not going to get anywhere with us today.

"I'm going to start with someone else. You guys are two sick people," he said, trying to look disgusted as he prepared to leave our room. "Learn to control yourself."

I was about to say I was sorry when more gas was released. The farting sound was drowned out by the sound of mine and Brett's laughter, as we looked at Jonas' face. He shut the door, but we saw him smiling as he walked out.

Although I didn't take many phone calls my senior year, there was one occasion when I answered the phone out of habit.

"Hey," I mumbled.

"Is this Jeff Boschee?" a female voice asked

"Yeah, what's up?" I said, automatically. Too late I realized it was not a familiar voice.

"Jeff, I just wanted to hear your voice and find out what you were like," she said.

I sighed into the phone, thinking to myself I had made a mistake answering this call. Now I was going to have to talk to someone I had never met. And the conversation would probably include all those questions I hated, about my love life and girlfriends.

"Well, now you know," I said, trying not too sound to encouraging.

"Don't hang up on me yet," she said, in a rushed voice "I actually want to talk to you for just a few minutes."

"About what?" I asked, trying to keep my voice flat and unemotional.

"Your personality," was the reply. "I don't want to talk about basketball or even a date. Just your personality."

I gave a short laugh into the receiver.

"Why would you care about my personality?" I asked. "We'll never meet."

I was trying to get this to end without being overly rude. But I was getting to that point where I just wasn't interested in talking to a detached voice anymore.

She replied, "You'd be surprised how many people wonder what Jeff Boschee is like. Not as a lover or boyfriend, but as a person. People look at you while you are playing or sitting on the bench. And they try to imagine what it would be like to know you."

I instantly thought this was going to be an attempt to get together, a way to try and become my new best friend.

"And you want to meet me and find out," I said, thinking I was finishing the thought for this girl.

"No, I don't," she said, in a voice that became matter of fact. "I think that would be useless. It would never happen, because you probably get asked that all the time."

"So what is it you want to talk about?" I asked, confused as to where this was heading.

"Just what is it that makes you tick. I want to know some parts of your personality that don't show while you are playing basketball. I can see determination and aggression. I want to know what is on the inside."

"Well, I don't know how you can do that without meeting me," I said. "I'm not good about talking on the phone and I don't usually talk to anyone for more than a couple of minutes. My friends know better than to try and call me just to talk."

"See, that's what I mean," she said, happily. "Now I know something about you that I would never have known from watching a game." She sounded proud of herself, as though getting this detail about me had been important. I realized that it probably was important to her. The whole conversation had been just talk in my mind, and quite honestly, it had been pointless. It was a waste of my time until she made that last comment.

"Why is this so important to you?" I asked, probably sounding frustrated and puzzled.

"I already told you. I want to know what you are really like as a person," she repeated, sounding a bit annoyed that I hadn't understood.

"I'll never figure out why that means so much to people," I said. "Why can't you just watch me play basketball without wanting to know me?"

"Well Jeff, someday you'll figure that out," she said triumphantly.

And then the phone clicked. No sound but a dial tone.

I was surprised. I must have sat on the sofa for a few minutes, staring out at the balcony of my apartment. This was one of the strangest conversations I could recall. It was not annoying nor was it long. I didn't have to try and get rid of the caller. Yet I felt as if I was being controlled, as though somehow this person had manipulated me into doing exactly what they had wanted.

Her comments stuck with me for a long time. How many people out there watching Kansas games wanted to meet any one of us? I always knew they wanted the autographs and obviously some wanted dates. Now there was a new group of people to think about, the ones who wanted to know what I was like. This seemed strange to me. I watched athletes play all the time, but never wanted to get to know them. I used to think about playing against them, but never actually hanging out with them or getting to know them.

I think that conversation led, in part, to the writing of this book. Hopefully the people who want to get to know what I'm like will have a better understanding after reading this. And for the girl who made that phone call: I still haven't figured out why this means so much to you.

The real puzzle for me as the year was winding down was the decision whether or not to go pro. The NBA is the ultimate, the peak of any basketball player's dreams. It's the final stop as you climb the ladder of basketball success. Everyone is supposed to want to be an NBA star.

I guess I'm not like everyone. My dreams are not in a direct order, and the dream I had always placed first was to play for Kansas. I wanted to be a college basketball player, be a Jayhawk, and then see how things went. I never had the NBA as my final stop. I'm not quite sure why that was.

Maybe it had to do with the fact that I'm only 6'1." There aren't a lot of guards my height playing in the NBA. I'm not a fan of sitting on the bench. I don't think I'd really enjoy being an NBA bench guy, the last off the bench when fans are streaming for the exits. Getting 3 minutes of playing time two nights a week is not my idea of fun.

I believe I could play at that level. I know I can shoot better than many guys who are in the league now. There is something about moving up there right now that is not appealing. Because of that, I never spent time thinking about getting an agent, never spent last summer thinking about where I wanted to play in the NBA. I wanted to play for Kansas and win a national title. When I thought about basketball last summer, that's where my mind went.

The key thing is that right now, I don't want to become an NBA player. I'm still burned out on the sport and the thought of working out for weeks after our season ends doesn't excite me. I don't want to have to fly to tryout camps this spring. I don't want to keep up the constant conditioning, keep shooting for hours a day and spend the entire spring in class or in the gym. When this season ends, I want to relax and enjoy life. I want some time to be me.

Bench support from the starters.

Is that wrong? Is there something that says I must continue to play ball? I don't think I should answer to anybody but myself. I have heard comments made to the effect that I owe it to my fans to keep playing. Nobody has the right to tell someone how to live their life. There is nothing wrong with people encouraging me to give it a try, to explore the possibilities. I appreciate that kind of support, that belief in my ability. I know those people are well intentioned.

It's the folks who want to continue to watch me play for other reasons that I can't understand. Looking at me is not the reason to come to games. Seeing my team is a great reason. I'm just one part of what made Kansas successful. I certainly am not the only reason we won games the past four years. I am part of a great team and a great program. That's our key to success. We all understand that it takes all of us to be successful. Coming to watch only me play, and not caring how the other guys do is insulting. It insults my teammates and implies that I'm above everyone else. None of us feels this way, so I don't think people should get that idea.

My career is at a crossroads right now. No matter to whom I've spoken, people are generally taken aback by my feelings about the NBA. I guess it's typical for most guys at this level of college athletics to try to make it in the pros. I suppose that means I'm not your typical guy. I just don't have the desire to do it.

Maybe I will get that desire back. I believe that if I take a year off, and start working hard next January, I will still be able to try for the NBA. I think if I refresh my mental self, I will be more of an asset to any team. Right now, I'm not the kind of player a coach would want on his team. I don't know how much I would put into trying my best at any other place than Kansas.

Next year will be different. I will have had time to get a clear look at my life. Being away from basketball, getting time to live as my friends live, having afternoons free and not being tied to any schedule but my own is something I want to try. This is how most college students live. I want to see how that is, to experience that kind of life. I'm young, I've got time to decide what to do with my life. That's exactly what I intend to do.

Chapter 8

Big 12 Conference Games
SPECIAL MEMORIES

The conference season was as tough as ever, but there were three games which stand out in my memory. The first was against Texas Tech. The main reason for that was their new coach. He was a man named Bob Knight.

The mere entrance of Coach Knight is something to behold. At his height he's an imposing figure, someone who simply has to stand on the floor to command respect. As he walks across the floor to the visitors bench, there is a sensation that someone important is here. He didn't say a word, simply stood there and watched us go through about a minute of our warmup. Yet we all felt something different about this game.

Actually, I had met Bob Knight seven years earlier, when I was a freshman in high school. A coach from Fargo took a group of basketball players to the Indiana University summer team camp. We played a few games and apparently Indiana assistant coach Ron Felling noticed me. After our games were over on the second day, Felling walked over to me, told me he liked the way I played and asked if I would be interested in coming to a morning shooting session the next day. I was excited about this and replied, "Sure I would. What time?" "Be back here at 8 a.m.," Coach Felling responded. I don't remember if I said anything else. I know I had trouble sleeping that night.

The next morning there I was, a 9th grader, working with the assistant coach from Indiana University on their home floor. I went through a series of shooting and ballhandling drills by myself, with

Coach Felling watching on the side in silence. Suddenly I sensed someone else standing on the far side of the gym, in the shadows. I stopped for a minute to rest and take a look. It was Coach Knight. Feeling the urge to really perform well, I pushed myself for the next 10 minutes, trying to be as perfect as I could. I noticed the two coaches talking at the end of the court, and then Coach Knight called me over and asked me to sit with him.

He was friendly and nice, nothing like I had heard or read. He talked with me about playing basketball, about the work ethic involved in becoming a success and about a few other topics. Knight told me he believed I had a great future in the sport, provided I kept on working at improving myself. He said that desire would make me a better player, and to believe in myself.

During my junior year of high school, Coach Knight started trying to recruit me. I talked with him once, and missed his calls a

Photo by Earl Richardson

Coach Bob Knight of Texas Tech.

few other times. It was flattering to be called by such a high profile person as Bob Knight. By then I wasn't interested in Indiana, having set my dreams on Kansas.

Now he was coaching at Texas Tech, taking over a program that was in the bottom half of the Big 12 conference. In his first season he had this team ranked in the top 25, and at the time we played them, had only lost 5 games. It looked to be a tough game.

Our defense was awesome that night, and we were on fire offensively. I seemed to be able to hit from anywhere, going 6 for 8 from the field. We blew Tech out of the gym, 108-81, and solidified our position as the team to beat in the conference.

After the game, Coach Knight sought me out before we left the floor. He walked up to me, shook my hand and put his arm around my shoulder for a moment. He looked me in the eye and told me that he felt I had a great career in college basketball. He flashed a smile and left.

I thought about this afterwards. It was a very nice gesture on Coach Knight's part to seek me out after his team had lost a big game. He never had to do that. People have opinions about him, formed by what is printed in the press. I've dealt with him and here's my opinion about Bob Knight: he's a decent man.

Personally, of all the towns in the Big 12, my least favorite is Stillwater. An odor that is a cross between manure and sewage seems to hang in the air outside. The hotel we stay at is the worst one in the conference. In my opinion the gym is my least favorite. It's not a place that favors shooters. As you can tell, I'm not fond of playing Oklahoma State on the road.

I woke up before the game this year feeling sick to my stomach. I had dry heaves which later progressed to diarrhea. I was shaky, felt damp but yet had a dry throat and couldn't eat anything all day. I drank lots of Gatorade and when we had our team meal, finally managed to get a double baked potato into myself. Considering all of this, what happened that night is almost ironic.

Oklahoma State was ranked 6th in the nation at the time. They had been having one of their best seasons in years, and we knew it would be a tough game. This turned out to be one of my best defensive games of the year. I hung with my man and kept the ball out of his hands for much of the first half. I seemed to have more focus on defense and felt more energy at that end of the court. But this was a night when an offensive play would stand out.

Late in the first half, we were out on a secondary break. Aaron Miles had the ball and was bringing in through the lane. He kicked it out to where I was standing on the left side of the baseline, near the corner. I caught it and everything seemed to flow just right. The ball left my hands with the spin my brother had taught me so many years earlier and it felt perfect. I saw the ball swish through the hoop, the net gently jumped up, and I moved back on defense, looking for my opponent.

At the next timeout, I was informed that I had just broken the Kansas record for three-point baskets, previously held by Billy Thomas. The shot from the corner was the 270th of my career. We returned to the floor and the game continued. The idea of setting the record was not in my mind.

We beat Oklahoma State 79-61 and it wasn't until I was on the bus headed back to the hotel that I had a chance to think about the record. Actually, I probably would not have thought about it if Brett Ballard hadn't made a comment about being in the presence of a record holder. That made me think.

On the bus back to Lawrence, I realized how awesome an achievement this was. Kansas has had so many great athletes, so many guys who could score. Records have never meant much to me. I don't keep trophies all over my apartment. Actually my mother has nearly every award I've ever received. Some are in boxes while others are displayed in the family room at home. I have exactly three trophies in my bedroom, and two are from high school.

The sense of history is what I felt that night. I was a senior, coming to the end of my career. Normally I don't tend to reflect very much on the past but tonight was different. Whether it was the length of the ride or just some unusual mood, I was thinking about how basketball had brought me to this point in my life. All those days back in North Dakota playing and shooting, working with my friends at becoming a better shooter, playing imaginary games against invisible opponents....how many guys have done the same thing? How lucky was I to be the one who set a school record?

Kids grow up and wonder if they will ever fulfill their dreams. You hope, wish and pray for things that, as time goes on, seem almost trivial. As a 20 year old, you would chuckle at how important some things seem to a 10 year old. It never enters a person's mind that similar dreams were once theirs. This was one of the first time those thoughts entered my mind.

I used to want to be as good a player as my brother Mike. I wanted to play on a team that traveled around the state. It was very important to me to be able to shoot the ball accurately from behind the three point line. If I could do that, I would be considered a good player, better than my friends who were having trouble getting the ball up to the rim. Those were very important topics in my life when I was ten. They aren't even issues today.

How would I feel about this record 10 years from now? The difference this time is that I never set a goal to break the KU record. When I was younger, those dreams became goals, something I worked hard to achieve. As I matured, the goals changed. The main focus became getting to a Division I program, specifically Kansas. And that's all I ever wanted to do: just start and play well for the Jayhawks. Setting the three point record just happened along the way.

It gives you a sense of pride to know you have reached your goals. A person gets more self confidence from being able to achieve what they have been striving to accomplish. To use a cliche, success does breed success. To some people, I was now a success because I had set a record. Yet I didn't really feel that way.

I'll never admit I wasn't proud of the record. I was and still am. It's great to know that my name is at the top of at least one list in this world. There is something else I considered when thinking about the 3-point record. This is a record for being a good shooter. It does tell that, but holding it does not tell whether or not I am a good basketball player. Shooting awards are great to hold. Being a complete player is what I'd like to become. If there is an award for that, I'd like to get it. That's a trophy I'd put right in the center of my home.

We were getting off the bus when Jeff Hackel, one of the managers, asked me, "Hey Jeff, where's the ball?"

"What ball?" I said, looking puzzled.

"You set the Kansas record tonight for 3-pointers. Where is the game ball?" Hackel said.

"Nobody gave me anything. I never thought about it," I replied.

"That sucks," Hackel said. "You'd think the least they could do is give you the ball you used to set a record."

I hadn't thought about it, but Jeff had a point. The record had been broken on the road. Oklahoma State might not have even realized that it happened. Nonetheless, to the best of my knowledge, there is nothing to commemorate that night. I know I'll receive something when the season ends, but my mother will have to settle for that.

My parents gave up an awful lot for me to become the player that I am today. I guess it's something that comes with getting older and I know that's something many kids are told by their folks. The point is, it's true. Unfortunately, you start to appreciate things long after they occurred. That's the case with my parents.

I won't say I was totally self-centered, but I never realized how much they had to sacrifice until I started to read stories in the paper. My folks came to 70 of my games during my KU career. They bought a new SUV right before my freshman season. In three and a half years, they put 96,000 miles on that vehicle. Virtually all of that was driving I-29 from Valley City to Lawrence.

They never took any other vacations. After my freshman season, they started to car pool with Kirk Hinrich and Nick Collison's parents, both of whom lived in western Iowa. Sometimes they would meet and all get into the Hinrich van, which could seat 8 people comfortably. Other times they would still drive the entire trip themselves.

There is some irony here. As players we ate in great restaurants and stayed in nice hotels. My folks ate bologna sandwiches and occasionally slept in the van to save money. On a few trips to road games, one family would rent the room and the other two would use the shower and facilities, just to economize.

They had some adventures as well. They were stranded at a rest area in Iowa when a blizzard struck. They had to rock the car until it cleared itself from a snowdrift, and then took the advice of a truck driver and waited out the storm. Amazingly, they still made it to Allen Fieldhouse in time for the tip-off.

My folks did come on some road trips which were vacations. I know they saved money for three years so they could accompany us to Hawaii for the Maui Invitational. They drove to Boulder to see us play Colorado and went with the Hinrichs and Collisons to New York my junior year.

I never knew some of these things until my senior year. It makes me feel special, to know that my parents love me so much to make these sacrifices just to watch me play basketball. I don't show my emotions very often, but I know what I would do if they were here right now.

Missouri has the most immature fans I've ever encountered in my college career. I'm not applying this label to everyone who is a fan of the Tigers. Many are just excited because it's Kansas coming to town. The people I'm referring to are those who get into the arena and decide to act as if they are three years old.

Much of this is not student body behavior. It's expected that college kids act crazy at times. Part of the fun in playing college basketball is seeing how the different schools try to get to us before, during and after a game. Whether it's some kind of chant (which is useless, since most guys will tell you they never hear once the game starts) or some other stunt, as a fan watching the game, this crowd involvement adds to the atmosphere of a college game.

At Missouri, it's different. I know Kansas and Missouri are bordering states. I'm aware of the bragging rights people claim when their state has the better team. In spite of that, I find it amazing how ridiculous some of the adults sitting around the court can behave before a KU-MU game. Men and women who appear to be at least in their 60's scream things at us during pre-game warmups. They sit literally at courtside, shouting comments about our appearance, our families and obviously our team. This never stops during the game. As I said, the mere fact that it's not students but elderly adults is what I find strange.

A man who appears to be in his mid-60's sits behind the basket every year. He does a routine with a black and yellow scarf, waving it and finally throwing it in the air while you are shooting a free throw. Thinking about it, fans at almost every school do something like this. However, at the games I've played in or watched on television, the ones waving towels or signs are students, not grandparents.

There has been a change in the style of ball Missouri plays in recent years. I know that in past years, some of the guys from Kansas have complained about a dirty style that was more common in games with Missouri than other Big 12 programs. I've got to say that if that was true, it's not anymore. My perception about Tiger teams the past three years is a finesse team rather than a physical style. There have not been any cheap shots I can recall from my games against Missouri. Maybe things are changing. Now if only their fans would grow up....

We were playing a game against Colorado, and time was running out. I caught a pass coming off a screen, and faced the basket, squaring up my shoulders. I released the ball and watched as it softly landed in the net, causing the twine to jump up as if it were cheering.

Waiting for a moment as Nick or Drew lose their defenders and get open underneath.

Kansas beat Colorado, due to that shot. The opportunity to hit a game winner doesn't come along often during a season and I was pumped. It's quite a feeling, something every kid dreams about while shooting around the basket at home.

It's hard to actually describe the feeling I get when I hit a three pointer. I love everything about it. The distance the ball travels makes everyone in the gym stop and watch. There is a feeling of suspense, the players on both teams wondering if this attempt will succeed. The fans in the bleachers collectively hold their breath, waiting to see if three more points will enter the scorebook. The moment of truth arrives, the ball goes in, and the crowd explodes with a huge increase in the noise level. It's great.

That's how the public perceives the shot. In my head and in my heart, I have a separate reaction. The shot itself is deflating to an opponent. I can remember playing against Iowa State this season, and hitting a three late in the game. Jake Sullivan was coming right at me, trying to block the shot. I got it over his hand, and when it went in, the look in his eyes said everything. He didn't race down the court afterwards, he sort of slumped a bit in the shoulders and his body language told me I had taken something out of him.

I believe the three pointer is the best shot in the game. The dunk can be spectacular and it's a great shot. But it can also fire up the opposition and make them want to try harder. At times, the dunk can backfire and the opponent will become more determined. The three point shot doesn't have that effect. It gets the home crowd into a game, but can silence a crowd on the road.

I always believe every three pointer I take will go in. There is a thrill I cannot explain, something that runs through my entire body when I connect on a shot. I have a sense of pride at my accomplishment but it's more the enjoyment and happiness that stick with me. Just thinking about making a three pointer causes me to feel good.

It's a tradition at most schools. A night is set aside to honor the seniors in the basketball program. This year the opponent was someone Kansas fans always love to beat: Kansas State.

I was not as concerned with the game this year. I believed we would beat K-State, and the feeling of a rivalry was just not there. The most important thing this year was that this would be Senior

Night. It was going to be the last time I ever played a game in Allen Fieldhouse.

I remember the first time I ever saw Allen Fieldhouse. I was awestruck. I had never seen so many fans for a basketball game in my life. The layout of the place, the bleachers on the floor and the seats above, the color combinations and the old gray walls, the windows from another generation and the banners suspended from the ceiling, all combined to make this a special place. It typified the word tradition.

There is no place I could imagine being better. More modern arenas certainly exist, and there are places with far more seats. The NBA would never play in a place like Allen Fieldhouse and that's part of their problem. This gym exists for basketball and the game is what is important, not a light show or oldies played to get the crowd aroused. At Kansas, the fans get worked up about the game.

The first game I ever saw here was on my recruiting trip. As the pregame introductions began and the student section began to cheer, I found myself getting goosebumps. I hadn't felt like this since my first game for Valley City, and this feeling was more intense. The band, the sound of the crowd and the Rock Chalk Chant at the end of the game combined to keep that feeling the entire night. It has never left me during the past four years.

I sat in my chair before the game looking around the locker room. The guys might have been more relaxed than at any time this year. It was like a party, with lots of conversation, music and laughter. Drew was his usual self, getting everyone loose by telling jokes in his own hilarious style. If there was one reason we played without a lot of tension this season, it was because of Drew Gooden. He manages to make everyone happy, and the freshmen especially responded to him. It dawned on me that the group of Aaron, Keith, Wayne and Michael will continue this locker room style in the future.

The locker room itself was something I never thought about until tonight. Maybe it hit me when I opened my locker and saw the gold nameplate inside the door. Two years ago it was decided to begin listing which Jayhawk had previously occupied each locker. Billy Thomas had been in my locker before I arrived at KU. Ironically, it was his record I had broken earlier this year.

I sat in my folding chair and looked around the room. Every guy on the team has a padded folding chair with their name emblazoned on the back, done in Kansas colors, in front of their locker. The seniors will get to keep this chair after tonight, along with the shorts we wear for every home game. The jerseys will be auctioned off at a charity event. The memories will stay forever.

There is an entertainment center that greets you as you enter the door. The large television is easily seen from any part of the room, whether we are watching film of ourselves or any regular TV show. The wood grained lockers with gold handles, the carpet with the Jayhawk in the center of the floor, everything about the room speaks of the class of our program. We might have an old exterior, but inside, this is a modern building.

Fans cannot get to this area. There is a keypad which must be programmed to enter the hallway where our locker room is located. The coaches locker room is down the hall from ours. Both ends of the hall are locked with large wooden doors. It's a safe haven for us, but also necessary if we are to get ourselves mentally ready for every home game.

Tonight, it wouldn't take much for me to pump myself up for the game. It was my last game at home. Four years earlier I had left Valley City, knowing I would never play another game in that gym. I thought I'd never experience that feeling again, a mixture of happiness and sadness that's hard to explain. You feel the thrill of knowing you're moving ahead with your life, yet you want to

Photo by Earl Richardson

The starters enjoy watching our teammates take it to K-State.

Giving my Mom a hug on Senior Night. My Dad is on the right, with glasses.

desperately hang on to the present for awhile longer. The pit of your stomach aches a bit, knowing that this moment will never return. It was like that for me tonight.

By the time I was thinking about what I would say, the game was over. We blew out Kansas State, 103-68, and everyone was in a great mood. The team had just completed the home season undefeated and now the six seniors were about to make our final walk across the floor in front of the fans.

Brett Ballard and Lewis Harrison were the first two guys to speak, and they were hilarious. Brett commented about how good the coaches had been and then hinted that he hoped all those nice comments would be remembered when they were thinking about who should get playing time in the tournament. Lewis opened with the best one liner of the night. He told the crowd," Don't worry, this speech will be about as long as my playing time has been this season!" The place erupted in laughter and the coaches were actually doubled over. Lewis took almost a minute to stop laughing himself.

This made me more relaxed. I knew I would be last, since I was the lone starter among the seniors. I expected an introduction from Max Falkenstien, the long time KU announcer, that would state the 3-point record I had set a few weeks earlier. The sound of the cheers are what caught me by surprise. They were so loud, I was suddenly nervous again. I started to pace back and forth as I spoke.

I thanked my friends who had come from North Dakota to see me in this final game. I think they knew how much I had needed their support, but I don't believe they understood how much they meant to me off the court. I never said as much that night, but I knew they had helped me overcome a lot more than a shooting slump. They had helped me finish my career at Kansas.

I went on to thank my teammates, the members of my family who were present, and finally got around to the most difficult person of all: Coach Williams. I started to choke up, and literally had trouble speaking at two different points while talking about him. I did get to say one thing I had always felt. "Coach," I said, "thanks for taking a chance on me." I had always known it was a gamble for him to recruit me over other more notable guards, especially guys who were quicker. I got to live my dream, and he was the person who made it come true.

I couldn't look directly at Coach when I was saying this. I would have lost it, and that's something I didn't want to do in front of all those people. When I saw the tape of the ceremony later, I noticed that Coach had the same look himself. I could tell on his face he appreciated what I said.

When we returned to the locker room afterwards, we assembled in our chairs for the post game comments. Coach Williams told us, "If someone placed one million dollars in front of me and told me I could have it if I were willing to trade what just happened on that court … if they said I could have a million dollars but never hear those comments from you guys … I'd tell them to keep their money." He glanced around the room at all of us, smiling and seeming to linger on the seniors for a moment longer. Then he walked out.

The next day Coach told someone that he couldn't look at me before the game. When he was going through our final pregame preparations he looked at everyone but me. He said he didn't want to break down in front of the guys. While I was speaking, he looked down or away from me, but never looked directly at me until I came to the part where I was addressing him.

I tried to think back to before the game but drew a blank. Coach

Holding the Big XII trophy for going 16 - 0 in the regular season. On my right is Brett Ballard, to the left is Lewis Harrison and Jeff Carey.

not looking at me while talking before a game is something I wouldn't focus upon or remember, unless he was in an angry mood. I went home and looked at the video tape my girlfriend made of the Senior Night speeches. Since I was speaking at the time, I had no way of knowing that Coach wasn't watching me, but it's true. The moments when the camera pans towards him, Coach Williams is looking at the floor.

Bags full of mail arrived weekly during my junior and senior years. There simply was not enough time for me to try and answer all of it. Between classes, practices and games, I was pretty tired. I wanted to get away from dealing with basketball day and night. Reading and answering the mail would only increase the feeling that I was talking about basketball all the time. I saved much of it, but never read many of those letters until after the season.

I know there are a lot of disappointed people out there. The mail usually contained requests for a picture or an autograph on a piece of paper. Sometimes the person would include their phone number and want me to call them. Reading about that, weeks after the fact, made me think of how they must have been waiting by the phone. I sure hope that wasn't the case, but I'll never know.

Long Shot: Beating the Odds to Live a Jayhawk Dream

A great many of my fan letters dealt with finding out more about what kind of person I am. The questions remind me of a game called 20 questions, where someone asks you personal things to try and determine your personality.

To all those people who wrote letters I never answered, I am sorry. However, if I could have combined the answers to some of those letters, this is probably what I would say:

Dear (name), I'm very glad you took the time to write to me. I will try to answer all of your questions as best I can. One of my best traits is my kindness. I'm the type of person who can empathize with other people. I like to think I always am kind to people. At least, I try to be. My worst trait is being a procrastinator. If there is a way to put things off, I usually find it. I have been known to wait until hours before an event or deadline to get started with something. I wish I could improve upon this.

A typical Jeff Boschee night could involve television. If I have nothing to do, I will just sit and veg out in front of the tube. I like to watch "Unsolved Mysteries"or shows involving sports. Most sports interest me. I also watch "Real World" on MTV. PlayStation games also interest me. My two favorites are "NBA GameDay" and "Cool Boarders." I play this in spurts. There will be a week where I get so into these games I can't do anything else. This will be followed by a month or two where I won't play any Play Station. It just depends on when the mood strikes me.

I am someone who tends to forgive people easily. Because I like to think I'm a kind person, I don't hold grudges. That doesn't mean I don't get mad. One thing that really annoys me is when people talk behind someone's back. Don't do that, tell people to their face if you have a problem. I know I would much prefer that to finding out someone is talking about me.

If I were going to a movie, I tend to like dramas, the type that keep you in suspense until the end. However, a good comedy is always a great choice. I am not into body piercing or tattoos. It's just not me.

Again, I'm sorry if I never wrote back. At least this letter might help.

Sincerely, Jeff

Chapter 9

The Big 12 Tourney

GETTING READY

I was going into the Big 12 tourney for the last time. Fans sometimes wonder about these types of things. How much did we want to win this tourney? We had just become the first team to ever complete an undefeated (16-0) Big 12 conference season. Should the team be concentrating on the NCAA title instead of a conference tourney title?

As an individual, I can tell you there aren't games I don't want to win. I don't look at what type of game it is I'm about to play. If I'm on the court, it's to win. People who think we analyze each game and consider the schedule beforehand are completely wrong. I know that sports talk radio is full of callers and commentators who will tell you different. It's not true. The locker room at KU is not a place where we sit and decide, "Should we save some of our energy for Oklahoma? Maybe we should take it easy on Baylor if we draw them in the first round?" That just doesn't happen.

One thing I did hear mentioned was true this particular season. The team was determined to win the Big 12 tourney for Coach Williams. It had been a few years since we brought home the title. We won the regular season with a perfect record, the first time that was ever accomplished. To do that and not win the title would be leaving something unfinished.

Coach Williams is a great coach. He possesses something that motivates people from within. You know he really cares about you as a person. Coach always says he's old fashioned and that's true. He is old fashioned in his beliefs and values. From what I've experienced, that's not a bad way to be.

I'm not an expert, but I do hope to become a college coach someday. With that in mind, I have some beliefs about what it would take to be successful as a coach.

I think the strongest attribute someone can possess as a coach is the ability to communicate to his players as people, not just as athletes. We are basketball players, but our lives do not end the minute we step off the court. Listen to some coaches. They can tell you the strengths and weaknesses of their players, of guys who played for them years before, and of the kids they are trying to recruit. Now ask that same coach to tell you three things about the player as a person. (Be sure to restrict the reply to non-basketball issues) You will be able to tell in an instant how this person communicates with their players. Any coach who cannot come up with a specific story about one of his players is someone who doesn't communicate well. After all, these are people he has spent an average of 15 or more hours a week dealing with on a daily basis. How can you spend that much time with someone and not know a thing about their lives, other than the fact that they can shoot the pull-up jumper?

High school and youth coaches should be even more conscious of this trait. Kids want to know the coach cares about them, not just their ability to play the game. My favorite coaches from my younger days were the guys who knew how to talk to me. Not only about basketball, but about things going on. I always felt they knew me as a person, and that made me want to play harder for them. Anybody knows you are more apt to work harder for someone you like than someone who just barks commands and expects obedience. Obedience doesn't mean the effort is there. Kids give an effort if the effort is appreciated. To demonstrate that, you have to communicate.

The other factor I believe a good coach should possess is the ability to teach the game with a team approach. Obviously coaches probably have a special area they prefer. Some coaches are defensive specialists, some teach shooting and some teach passing. The key to this is teaching how it all fits together to create a successful team.

Coach Williams was the type of coach who put everything together. We learned when to take the best possible shot, when to make certain types of passes, and how to play a style of team defense that allowed us not only to defend, but to get into transition and score before our opponents knew what happened. Our running game was not just the result of speed. It was the result of our defensive pressure, and our ability as a team to know where each of us was supposed to be after we got the ball.

I won't tell you I was perfect in my relationships with my coaches. I liked every coach I have had, and owe a lot to those men who helped me achieve my goals as a player. Everyone from my AAU coach Dave Thorsin through my brother Mike helped me get to the level where I could play for Coach Williams at Kansas. But that doesn't mean there were moments when I wasn't totally receptive to what I heard or was told by the coach.

One day at practice, I hit a shot I thought was pretty good. As soon as I turned to get back on defense, Coach commented on why it was not the right thing to do. I'm thinking to myself, "You jerk, what do you want from me?" It made me mad and I took out my anger on defense. Suddenly I realized why Coach criticized me. I was now playing more aggressive defense. My anger was being channeled into that part of my game. Coach Williams was making me a better player, motivating me in a way he knew would work in my individual situation.

He knew me as a person from our conversations. He knew how to get the most out of me, and use that to make our team better. Looking back, it's why he's one of the most successful coaches in college basketball. It's why I became a better player. And it's something I would try to do should I ever become a coach.

I like coaches who have a sense of humor. Coaches have to be able to laugh at themselves, and with the rest of the team. We work hard at practice and I like it when there are moments when someone can just loosen up and enjoy things. Right before we were going to play in the Big 12 tourney, Coach Williams decided to have the post players practice perimeter moves, and the perimeter players worked at being post players. There was Nick Collison, trying to come off screens and pop three-pointers, while Aaron Miles and I were working on a drop step moves to the hoop. The mere thought of what would happen to me should I try to post up someone from Oklahoma had the guys laughing, and the sight of Jeff Carey dribbling as though he would bring the ball up against full court pressure kept us loose for the entire afternoon.

Some coaches can drive players out of their system, and some have routines that are difficult to follow. This past year, we played

Iowa State at home in February. We were surprised to arrive at the gym around 5 p.m. and see the Cyclone team going through a full two hour practice. By the time they were finished, they had to be tired. Two hours later, they were taking the floor to play us in a Big Monday, ESPN game. I felt sorry for them and knew that I could never play in a system like that.

Coaches should assemble a staff that can deal with every aspect of the game. To me, that also includes the players needs as people, not simply as athletes. Our coaching staff at Kansas is excellent. Coach Neil Dougherty is the most knowledgeable basketball man I've ever known. He can give you such insight, sees the little things that separate good players from great ones, and knows how to teach the game. Coach Dougherty is especially good with the guards, since that's his former position. He's in great physical shape, works out more than some players I've met, and stresses that we remain in top condition. He's always yelling "Sprint!" and makes sure we run from drill to drill. Every single guy on the team feels the same way about him. He knows basketball.

Coach Joe Holladay is more laid back. He's the one who is more into the players as people, but he also works us almost as a perfectionist. Coach Holladay is the one coach I hated to hear get mad at practice because he has what I consider a nagging voice.

Once, we were working on our 1-3-1 matchup zone defense. I was moving out too soon, turning it into a 2-2-1, which would never work in our defensive scheme.

"Jeff!" Coach Holladay said, "you're coming out too soon. Stay on the wing."

"Okay coach," I said.

We ran the defense again, and I was concentrating. I screwed up again,, coming out too soon.

"Jeff! Jeff!!" Coach Holladay yelled. "What did I just say? What did I just say?"

As he was repeating this, his voice began to rise to a higher pitch. It started to get that nagging tone.

There was nothing I could say. I was screwing up big time. But I was still getting irritated because of his voice. Coach Holladay works us hard, going over detail after detail until we get things correct. It's one of the best parts of our game at Kansas, being good at the little things which win ballgames.

The newest member of the staff is Coach Ben Miller. He joined the program my sophomore year. Coach Miller is the quietest of the staff at practice. However, he's the one the guys know they can go to with questions about almost anything. One thing that Coach Miller has started is having the team over to his house for a barbecue when the season is over. It's a pretty relaxed atmosphere and a good way to get together one final time before the school year ends.

I believe the most important things a player should consider when choosing where they want to play college ball is the coach. And not his reputation. Look at the style of the man. After all, the coach is going to be the most important person in your life for the next four years.

Todd Kappelmann was talking in the locker room after an especially long practice. "I just realized something," he said. I was bent over, untying my shoes and automatically asked him, "What's that?"

Todd said, "I used to dream of being on the basketball team when I was a regular student."

He paused for a second.

I looked at him and asked, "And now?"

"Now I'm on the team and think about all the free time I'd would have if I were a regular student," Todd replied.

Brett Ballard was listening and said, "You know, there are days when I feel the same way. I'd just like to have a little more time to myself."

I added a final thought. "Sometimes I wonder what free time would be like."

This is a dilemma facing the college basketball player. I think it's one of the worst parts of being a college athlete. To be good, you must continually practice. However, there are days when practice is something you almost dread. The time involved is longer than many people realize.

During the season, the NCAA has a regulation stating practices can not take up more than 20 hours per week. At the end of every week, I had to sign a sheet of paper stating that Kansas stayed within that limit. The managers always made certain that the senior captains signed that document.

I never realized how long practices would be when I first came to Kansas. I think every high school kid thinks practice is going to be about 90 minutes long, and even then they get bored by mid-season. It was probably the hardest adjustment I had to make, and even by my senior year it was still difficult at times. I could relate to what Todd was saying because I had the same thoughts on occasion.

We practice for about 3 hours per day. We lift weights for about one-half hour 3 days a week, and we do this before practice. During the season the weights are mostly to work our legs. This obviously makes practice harder by the second hour, since your legs are tired from lifting. It does make us stronger as the season wears on, and was probably a key ingredient in the style of game we were able to play. We also did some light work on maintaining our upper body strength, but not to any great extent.

Another point which might surprise fans was the fact we practiced on Sundays during the Big 12 season. If you think about it, we had to do this. We play games on Saturdays and Mondays in our conference. Thus the only way to correct things from the Saturday game, and to prepare for Monday is to practice the day in between. It's logical but many people are surprised. I guess they just assume Sunday would be a day off.

Coach Williams adapted to the teams he coached during my years at KU. By my senior year, he was changing as the year went on. We actually saw practice time grow shorter as the year continued. Coach said he trusted us more than any team he had ever coached. He demonstrated that by having lighter practices at times during January and February. It was a wise decision, as this team tended to work harder on those short days. We seemed to know that we had less time, so we tried to pack as much in as we could.

It's also easier on you mentally when you realize that not every day is going to be the same. Long practices might sound good to some fans, but when you are on that floor for hours, you start to lose concentration. This isn't good for a team and it destroys the preparation the coaching staff is trying to instill. I believe having altered his practice style my senior year was one of the key factors in our having such a great season. I know I enjoyed things a lot more than in previous seasons.

I'd spoken with former Jayhawks about how Coach Williams has changed through the years. The most striking difference is his practice methods. Some of the guys from ten years ago, people like Rex Walters and Greg Ostertag, said things were so much easier now. I don't know if I'd agree with the word "easier". I think the best word to use is "shorter." The length of time we spend on the floor has decreased from past years. It's actually decreased during my four years at Kansas.

Those guys used to talk about spending two hours on the floor. This was in addition to the weights, drills, and other parts of a KU practice. During my senior year, practices generally followed this format:

5 minutes of working on our shooting form
10 minutes of individual work
Gather at center court to hear the point of emphasis for the day
Work on fast break drills
Work with dummy offense or dummy defense
(This would simulate the coming opponent)
At this point, practice would actually begin
45 minutes of intense, full speed practice.

Don't think everything wasn't at full speed. It was, especially with Coach Dougherty present. Nonetheless, the final 45 minutes was at game intensity. We'd be diving for balls, going as hard as we could to the hoop, boxing out with elbows and bodies flying. We held nothing back when it was time for the actual practice to begin.

In some ways we were lucky there were no injuries during the season. Considering how we practiced, it's kind of amazing that we escaped without more than a few normal bumps and bruises. Still, I believe this was part of the secret of our success in my senior year. We practiced well because Coach restored the fun to practice.

Reporters have a difficult job interviewing me. I'm not talkative by nature, have a hard time opening up and don't like answering questions from people I don't really know. There is nothing personal about this. I am very grateful for the attention I receive. Since I first came to Kansas, I think I've had problems talking comfortably with the press.

When a request comes for an interview, it usually is done through the Sports Information Director. The SID will contact whomever the press wants to interview and let them know about this. Kansas lets

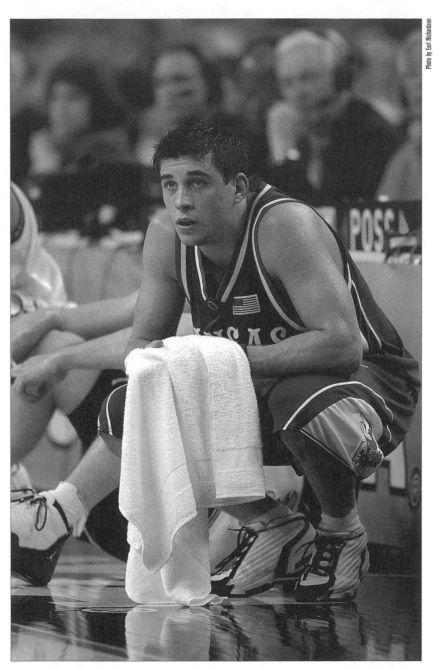

Getting ready to report in, after one of the infrequent rests I took during games. I played more minutes than anyone else my senior year.

each of us decide whether or not we want to meet with the press, or even receive the phone call, if that's how the session is to be conducted. Any time spent with the media is handled this way.

I generally shy away from interview requests. I guess I don't think details about the decisions made during a game make an interesting story. What could I have to say that would change what happened in the game that just ended? I never understood why reporters would ask me about a shot during a game. I can't understand why people find that sort of thing interesting to read. If I told them I felt I could make a shot, and I had missed that same shot, what good did I accomplish by making that statement to the press? Will it cause the shot to go in, now that the game is over? Isn't it logical to assume the reason I took a particular shot is because at that moment, in the flow of the game, I felt I could make it? I don't think I'm going to take a shot I thought I would miss. Now that would be something to read. "Boschee decides to take shots he knows won't go in."

I'm not blaming the reporters for this. It's something people want to know. Fans watch a game and replay it, looking for things that happened to change the course of the game. They analyze decisions we made in a split second and then try to figure out why we did those things. Where they are wrong is in thinking we also analyzed our moves before we made them. It can't happen in basketball. The game moves too fast, decisions are made often on instinct, through repetition in drills or simply from playing the game for years. We know one another as players from the hours we spend practicing together. We anticipate one another's moves or tendencies and react accordingly. It might be good if we could analyze our moves. To do that, however, we would have to know what the other team is going to do, and that's impossible.

Questions about my personality or my life off the court are a different matter. I don't get those as often as you might think. However, I don't like to talk about my private life. I was never anxious to do those type of interviews. If that's the direction the reporter wanted to go, I probably said no to the request. If I found myself suddenly involved in one of those discussions, most likely I gave short answers, without going into any details.

Probably the biggest thing that bothered me about post game interviews was the constant repetition of topics. I would get asked the same questions over and over. I realize the people asking things

were most likely not present when the question was asked earlier, but it still bothers me to repeat myself. I'm not patient with this type of thing, and I tried my best to hide that fact. The easiest thing for me to do was simply keep the answers brief and hope the press would move on to someone more talkative, like Drew or Nick.

As my senior year drew to a close, I started to relax. It seemed as though the success of our team and the mood of the locker room was rubbing off on me. I found myself answering in full sentences and actually enjoying being interviewed. I wish I could have been this way earlier in my career, but at least I was able to enjoy it now. Little did I know the best was yet to come.

Chapter 10

The NCAA Tournament
FIRST STEPS

I couldn't wait. We were one of the favorites to win. After three years of disappointment, I felt really good about the NCAA tournament. In past years we had good teams, but looking back on things I could see why we lost. There was something not quite right about each team in my previous three years. It could be the way we entered March, the way I felt at the time, or just something in the air. The feeling was different this time.

We were an experienced team. We had one of the nations' premier players in Drew, one of the top big men with Nick, Kirk was playing the best ball of his career and I was the senior with experience. Aaron had emerged as our fifth starter, and with Keith, Jeff Carey, Brett Ballard and Wayne Simien coming off the bench, we were deep. The scoring was the highest in the nation, our defense was tough and we had learned a lot this season. I felt as though we should win it all.

The balance in my life was good. I had learned how to take basketball and put it in its proper place. I had finally come to understand what my brother had told me four years earlier. I was using basketball, it wasn't using me anymore. I had decided to finish the season with as much effort and desire as humanly possible. I knew that after this year was over, I'd be taking time off. For all I knew, this was the end of my career. That motivated me in a way that's hard to explain.

It's not that I needed motivation. Heck, I'm a competitor who hates to lose. I never found myself not wanting to play a game of basketball. That's not what I mean. I guess it's the thought of finality, the thought that I will never play another college basketball game if we lost. The goal had always been to play college basketball at Kansas. The realization that this dream was coming to an inevitable end was sinking in. I wasn't quite sure how to handle that.

The first round games were being played in St. Louis. Under the new format this year, some teams were going to be playing what amounted to local games in the early rounds. Kansas was thus placed in a location which allowed many fans to drive to our opening game. We certainly would have the crowd on our side.

The room assignments placed me in a single room for this trip. That was just as well, since I was not in a sociable mood. I was not nervous at all, and neither were the rest of the guys. We felt anxious, we wanted to get started, to get on the court and play.

Holy Cross was the opponent and we knew virtually nothing about them. Coach gave us the scouting reports and we walked through a few things they liked to do. But this was not a team we had seen on television this year and sometimes that leads guys to getting strange thoughts about an opponent. It probably worked against us in the opening minutes.

We played a stupid game and were outworked by Holy Cross. There is no other way to state it. I was as guilty as anyone and right before the half, disaster struck. Kirk went down with an injury, and at the time, it seemed pretty severe. We went in at halftime and tried to recover. I don't even know if we were ahead or behind.

Coach told us we needed to start playing our game. We were listening, but I had the feeling many of the guys were thinking about Kirk. As the second half began, I knew we were in for a struggle. They had a different look in their eyes this half. It was a more confident appearance, an attitude that said, "Bring it on. We can take your best shot."

Our fans seemed frustrated. You could hear it in the sound of the crowd at every free throw, in the way they seemed to cheer. It was not support as much as an imploring sound, telling us to please play KU basketball the way they had seen it done all season. They would have been surprised if they knew what was going on each time we huddled on the floor.

I could sense it in my teammates. We were starting to doubt our ability to win this game. Each time we gathered during the second half, there were blank looks in their eyes, expressionless faces staring at one another. It was a scary moment and I couldn't think of a thing to say that would snap us out of it. I felt I had to start scoring, believed if one of us took charge it would bring us back to take control of this game.

Drew became the man. He never said anything, just took control of the game. I thought to myself, "he's proving why he's NBA material. He's playing like the best big man in the country." It was impressive to watch. Then Aaron Miles hit a big shot and Holy Cross faded a bit.

I hit a three and as was getting back on defense, I looked at the guy I was guarding. He seemed to lose a step and I had the feeling he was not trying as hard. Maybe it was just wishful thinking, but I thought to myself that between Aaron and my shots, we had taken something out of them. They knew they could not handle Drew, and now the rest of us were starting to contribute. They were finished.

Sometimes it's better to keep quiet about an official's call.

Afterwards, the locker room could not be described as happy. We had won the opening game but were extremely disappointed in ourselves. Coach didn't have to say anything to us about our performance. We all knew it had not been good. We were experienced enough to realize the level of competition would get better at each stop.

There was an underlying worry, different from anything we had dealt with all season. Kirk's injury was more severe than we had thought. If he couldn't play against Stanford, how would we do? I didn't know how to stop the guys from thinking about it. This was a form of group self-doubt and I hated it. I'd waited four years to be on a team this good, and I didn't want to see everything fall apart now.

I went back to the hotel and laid on my bed. Basketball was starting to dominate my thoughts again, and I didn't like it. This is what had caused me so many problems two years before. It may surprise you to read this, but at that moment I decided to just forget the NCAA's and watch T.V. So that's what I did.

The next morning I felt better. I woke up, went down to breakfast with the team and we headed over for our practice. Coach had been having light practices the latter part of the season, and today was no exception. We went through a brief walk through of Stanford's tendencies.

Coach has the scrimmage team run through the plays of our opponents. It's not for us to memorize, but simply a way for us to see how they might come at us. There is no way to truly scout an opponent in one day. Our coaching staff knows this, so their main goal is to give us a sense of familiarity. We might be able to recognize something tomorrow against Stanford that will allow us to gain an advantage. If it's the one play that produces a one point victory, it was worth it.

The most useful tool in getting us ready for Stanford came from an unexpected source. One of their top players, Casey Jacobsen, gave an interview to CBS after their victory over Western Kentucky in the opening round. Jacobsen told a reporter, "After watching Kansas, they aren't as good as I thought. We all feel they're beatable." I don't think he knew how we would take it. I never got the impression he was being cocky or trying to demean us. It was a response to a reporter's question and he answered it honestly. Considering how we had played against Holy Cross, I probably would have said the same thing.

But the guys on the team were ticked off. The coaches never taped it to the wall or anything like that. They never had to. I think it was Keith who said something about it first, then it spread and soon all of us had something to say about Jacobsen's comments.

Next, the print reporters got into the act. There were stories doubting whether we could win without Kirk. Now I know Kirk is an important part of the team. But how does that make guys like Aaron or Keith feel? Not to mention myself, Drew and Nick. It's basically saying we aren't much of a team without Kirk and that also served to irritate us. Kirk never felt like he was indispensable, he's not that kind of guy. He was just as mad as the rest of us about what everyone was saying about Kansas. We had played one game in the tourney, done a poor job of executing our offense and suddenly people were writing us off. It got us mad.

Stanford never knew what hit them. Jacobsen's comments motivated us more than anyone would have expected. This might have been the most physical game we have played all year. I know that Nick was getting rough with their big men, and I found myself trying to physically go after people on defense. As a team, I honestly felt we pushed them around, something people don't associate with Kansas basketball.

I was angry, far more than I ever felt going into a game. What people were saying, what the press was writing and what Stanford seemed to feel about our team was insulting. We were the number one team for a time this season. We had been in the top 5 all year. We were the highest scoring team in the nation. How could anyone believe it was all a fraud? How could people say that because of one injury we would fold up and go home?

This might have been my best game of the entire NCAA tourney. I hit 5 threes and had 5 assists. I felt I shut down my man on defense and contributed an attitude which carried over to everyone on the team. We dominated this game from start to finish. We were moving on to the Sweet 16 for the second year in a row.

The flight back to Lawrence from St. Louis was bumpy. As I said earlier, I'm not a good traveler when I'm in an airplane. However, I discovered on this trip our strength coach, Jonas Sahratian was worse than me. Jonas was sweating after only ten minutes, and his head would snap from side to side at every bump in the air. There were times when he reminded me of one of those bobble head dolls, and his eyes would get real wide when he felt the plane drop even for a second. It was hilarious.

The team plane landed at Topeka airport that night. We fly on a private charter during the NCAA tourney, and you might be surprised at who's on the plane. The team and coaching staff get to sit in the first class section, as you'd expect. However, there are alumni who buy seats just to have the privilege of flying on the same plane as us. These people sit in the coach section, along with the cheerleaders. Throughout the tournament we will share our flights, as has been the case during all four of my seasons at Kansas.

As we left the plane and began to walk through the terminal, it became apparent how fanatical our fans had become. People were handing us flowers, cards and other assorted items. There weren't many autograph requests this time, just heartfelt displays of support from people of all age groups.

I never cease to be amazed how wonderful our fans are at Kansas. When I think that these people are willing to come to an airport on Sunday night and stand in lines, waiting for us to arrive, it just blows me away. I don't know how early they got there, but judging from the amount of people I'd guess the ones in front may have been holding their spots for possibly two hours or more. And they did that just to hand guys like me a card, a flower of simply to say "keep up the good work" or "way to go, Jeff." They are really great people.

A story appeared at the time of the first round game that still amazes me. A woman in Kansas had just given birth to a baby girl and the story claimed she and her husband were going to name the baby after me. I can't imagine anything more flattering than this. Our fans are the most incredible people anywhere in the United States.

The girl would be named Ashley Boschee. At first I didn't take the story seriously. It sounded like a joke that Nick Collison would play on someone. When reporters started to ask me about it, I realized this was not a joke. It was an honor.

People have asked me if I feel I will be a legend someday. I wonder what a legend is. To me, a legend is someone who has done something nobody else could accomplish. At Kansas, Wilt Chamberlain is a legend. Mention his name and everyone knows who you are talking about. People of any age know something about him or have a mental picture about him. I doubt if that's the case with me.

Penetrating the defense.

I've been told I'm famous. Again, I have to disagree with this. I might be recognizable. I'd agree with that word because I feel it's true. My face is on television, my picture is on posters and websites, so I am a person fans of Kansas basketball would recognize. But that's not the same as being famous. To be famous, you should have done something that will last for decades, even a century. Those who have performed great deeds are famous. Shooting a basketball doesn't really stack up to what I would call a famous act. I'm proud of what I've done at Kansas and in my entire career, but I don't think it makes me a famous person.

Am I going to be a famous Kansas basketball player? That's up to the fans to decide. I could believe that I will somehow be remembered in this area. I know I became a better player here during my four years. I think there is more to me than just being a 3-point shooter. I improved my game, became the Big 12 leader in assist to turnover ratio, and learned to be a smart defender. Those things make me a better all around basketball player. Maybe I'll be famous because of that.

For now I'm content with the honor of having someone name their baby after me. I received a picture of this cute little girl a month after the season ended. I kept it and it's now in a scrapbook. Maybe I'll be lucky enough to see how Ashley looks a few years from now. And maybe someday, she'll become a famous legend.

Chapter 11

Sweet 16

BREAKING THROUGH

After the first two victories, practices became short and quick. Coach Williams felt we were at the peak of our conditioning and believed we would perform well. He was demonstrating that faith by going for no more than 30 minutes all week. On Monday, we had nothing more than a shoot around. We were coming off a good win over Stanford, and there were some sore bodies. Rather than risk anything, and considering that Kirk was still healing, Coach opted to take it easy.

Tuesday and Wednesday were days with 2 separate 30 minute sessions. We walked through some things we needed to go over considering Illinois, and worked hard both days. Quick practices don't mean easy. We put a great deal of effort into those shorter practices. I know that in my case, I wanted to be ready and wanted to be playing two more weeks. There was no way I'd consider taking it easy now. I think all the guys felt the same way. Coach was demonstrating faith in us, a belief we would work extremely hard to win it all. We were so tied to his thoughts that we picked up on that and gave him our best efforts.

During this time, classes were not being held. This year we were fortunate in that the schedule for NCAA games fell at a time when Spring Break occurred. The first week of the tourney, I missed two days of class when we left for St. Louis. This week was the break, so the campus was pretty deserted. If we were to win, we would miss three days during Final Four week. All told, a total of only 5 class days would be affected by our getting through the NCAA tournament. That probably surprises people who look at the month of March as completely lost to basketball players. That's not the case.

We took a plane to Madison, Wisconsin on Thursday, to get settled in and prepare ourselves for our biggest challenge yet. Illinois was the team who had eliminated us the year before at this exact same point. We would be playing on Friday night, in a setting favoring Illinois. Wisconsin is a Big 10 school, so Illinois had played there once every year. It's only a two hour drive from Chicago, so we knew there would be many more fans supporting them, simply due to the close proximity of the states.

My roommate was Brett Ballard, a great guy and one of the seniors on our team. Brett was originally a walk-on, but worked hard and became one of the top 9 guys on our team. He accumulated quite a few minutes this season, and it was helpful, especially when Kirk went down in the Holy Cross game. Brett is quite a talker, and as he gets more excited, the pace of his conversation quickens. I swear he can get more words into a few seconds than others can get in half-minute. He would be a good person to have to talk with this time, since I like to keep my mind off games until we get to the arena.

I'm not the only one who takes this approach. Drew and Keith spent a good deal of their time in the hotel playing the X-Box game system. I think it was Drew who brought it along, but things like this show how this team approached the game. We were not nervous at all going into the NCAA, and I swear we became more relaxed as we won more games. I know that's not the way the press portrays things. Many fans seem to think we sit and dwell on the game as it approaches, and I guess that has been the case on some other KU teams. This group liked to take things loose and easy. If anything, people might have misunderstood and thought we really didn't care. Nothing would be further from the truth.

Sometimes we played jokes on one another during this time. The previous week we were staying at the Union Station Hotel and Jonas Sahratian decided to get me going. He called my room once shortly before midnight, disguised his voice and asked, "Is this Mr. Boschee?" I tentatively answered, "Yes?" "Can you come down to the lobby and sign some balls?" he asked. I still hadn't caught on and became irritated that fans were pestering me late at night in my room.

"Who the hell gave you this number?" I demanded, in a not so calm voice.

"I just wanted you to sign some basketballs for me," he said, still disguising his voice

"Don't call this damn number again," I said. I slammed down the phone in disgust.

A few minutes later, Jonas called back. "Mr. Boschee, can we talk?" he said, still in the disguised voice. Before I could answer, he began laughing hysterically in the phone and I knew I had been had. As I realized what had happened, I started to laugh as well. "I'll get you for this," I told Jonas as I hung up the phone.

Illinois posed a problem unlike any other team we had faced. They were big and physical, more so than the normal team. The Big 10 plays a style of basketball unlike other conferences. Banging bodies on the inside, a lot of shoving and pushing, it's something you learn to expect when you play their teams. Illinois had stocked up on guys who were in the 240-260 pound range. It would be a test for us.

Since the loss last year, we had been told why we lost by the media. We were soft, we got physically beaten up, we weren't tough enough to beat Illinois. As with Stanford, it was something that got us angry. I know that Illinois is physical, but I also know I was not assaulted on the floor. I know that I didn't shy away from contact, that I was not intimidated by them the previous year. Yet, I was accused of all these things, as were my teammates.

Nick and Drew took this to heart. They were insulted at being virtually called "sissies" and Kirk in his quiet way was just as mad. Only Aaron and Keith were exempted from this, being freshmen, yet there were comments made about how, as Jayhawks, they were going to play the same way.

We took the floor for warmups, knowing that Illinois believed this. If you hear these stories enough, you tend to wonder if some of it isn't true. It would serve to help their confidence. We had to take that away from them right from the start.

I was guarded by Cory Bradford, just as it had been the year before. Most of the matchups were the same, since we were two teams with returning veterans. They had been a Final Four team, and were highly thought of at the start of the season. However, it had been a long season for Illinois and we realized this was not the same team we had lost to last year. Same people, different attitude.

The first half found us fighting to stay above water. We came out too aggressively, trying to shed the "soft" image, and found ourselves in foul trouble. Kirk, Nick and Drew all picked up three fouls before the half. At one point, Nick was whistled for two fouls within a 90 second span. Kirk dove for a ball and nailed an Illinois guy in the process. This was a double-edged situation. While we were proving to them we would not back down, it was costing us precious minutes from our starters.

At halftime, Coach told us to execute our offense. We were playing very tough "D," it was keeping us in the game and we were aggressive. However, we had become sloppy on offense and let Illinois stop us from doing what we do best: score. In the second half, we took better shots and one of those tournament moments occurred. Keith Langford came in and had the best game of his freshman season. I think he scored 19 points, but more importantly he gave us a spark that had been missing. Illinois seemed to be surprised, as if they had not expected him to do much, and the rest of us fed off Keith's energy. Aaron and Wayne Simien contributed 16 points between them and the freshmen class had helped rescue us.

It was close right to the end. We were up 71-69 and I was fouled. I thought I could seal this win, but missed the front end of a one-and-one. There were 22 seconds left and I tried to take my anger at myself out on defense. I stuck as tight to Bradford as possible, but it was their star Frank Williams, who took the shot to try and tie the game. He missed, Keith rebounded and was fouled. Fittingly, he sealed the win with two free throws.

It was about the time of the NCAA Sweet 16 that an article first appeared in some newspapers across the country, comparing our team to a boy band. Reporters noticed the girls who surrounded us wherever we went. Stories also mentioned how fans waited for us after the games, sometimes for an hour, just to get an autograph. They made us out to be the college basketball equivalent of 'NSync.

While the fans have always waited for us after games, the national press has never seemed to notice. It was like this before I got here, and fans will continue to wait now that my playing days are over. During my campus recruitment visit, Ryan Robertson had told me, "The fans here are the greatest. You've never seen anything like it. Wait until you try to leave the locker room after your first home game."

It seemed as though I had a larger share of female admirers than some of the other guys. At times, it became a topic for the guys to kid me about. "Everybody knows that Boschee's got all the women," Kirk Hinrich slyly told some reporters. He knew they would write it, and he also knew how much I didn't want it to be known. During my senior year, that only grew as the victories increased. Suddenly there were girls everywhere, and it didn't stop when the games were over.

I had always gotten some phone calls, but they seemed to increase in number as my Kansas career progressed. Some days the phone would start ringing at 8 in the morning, and it wouldn't stop until midnight, or until we took the phone off the hook. Many of the calls were from females, just wanting to talk or hear how my voice would sound.

There were offers of all kinds, from dates to sex. Once a woman came up to me and asked if we could have a word privately. She told me she wanted to take me home, take off my clothes, throw me in bed and make passionate love to me all night! The fact that she seemed to be 15 years older than me and was wearing a wedding ring didn't seem to matter to her. Another woman, closer to my age, was more blunt. She said when she was done with me, I'd know she was the best I ever had.

Anyone I was with had to endure a lot of this. I could be out somewhere and girls would come up to me and start talking, acting as if nobody else were there. In some ways, it was very flattering to be the subject of this much attention. In other ways, it became a pain, because I knew I could never sit and talk with my friends. Some guys liked this. "Hey, Jeff, I need a date. Let's go somewhere so I can meet some girls when you do" is the kind of comment my friends would make. Jeff Hackel wanted to buy my car so that girls would think I was driving it. That way, when they followed the car, at least he'd have a better chance of meeting them.

Basketball players certainly aren't the only athletes who get this attention. It was something new to me, because as a high school player nothing like this had happened. People told me about it, but until it started I never really believed it would continue with me.

Nailing a three against Oregon in the Elite Eight game.

Oregon was the first team in the tournament that scared me. I looked at them as a mirror image of us, a team that ran, shot well, played good transition defense and could rebound. I was worried about them. I generally tried to put opponents out of my mind, but Oregon kept coming back to me.

As most players do, I watched a lot of college games on ESPN and Fox Sports Channel. The teams from the east are always on, and our conference, the Big 12, is part of Big Monday on ESPN. However, the Pac-10 teams are only seen on Fox Sports. This past year, that channel was not available in Lawrence. Most of us were not as familiar with Oregon or for that matter with Stanford. We heard about Oregon, read things in magazines and on the Internet. Actually seeing their style would have been helpful.

The coaches tried their best to get us ready for this game. The reality of it was we were playing against ourselves. Oregon was Kansas with different personnel. In some ways, that would make it easy. In other ways, it was a scary thought.

This was a Sunday game, and that meant we already knew Oklahoma and Indiana had advanced to the Final 4. Oklahoma making it put some pride on the line. We had been the regular season champs, the team to beat all season long. Then, the Sooners had upset us in the Big 12 tournament final. We couldn't fall short in getting to the NCAA finals. We had to win this game.

I was so pumped up I couldn't believe it. For some reason I noticed I've been more relaxed since we began playing the NCAA games. This has been the case every year. Today was no exception. I was ready, I was anxious and I wanted to get this game underway. The rest of the guys seemed to be the same. Oregon was going to be a team of dead Ducks.

We exploded out of the gate, taking a 9-2 lead early, and never looked back. We ran the break, our transition defense was awesome, and they couldn't find an answer. In our short practice on Saturday, Coach Williams had emphasized getting back on defense. To get us ready, Coach had the Red team never take the ball out of bounds after a basket. If the Blue team scored, they just threw it downcourt. It forced us to get back, and we seemed to do a pretty good job of it by the end of practice. It was smart planning on Coach's part. Oregon never beat us down the floor all day.

The final score was 104-86. There was something truly satisfying about this win. As a team, we always believed in ourselves. I never felt as good about a team as I had this year. The guys were loose, never took things too seriously and responded to whatever happened all year with a relaxed attitude. We had nothing to prove to ourselves. We knew we were a good team.

What this game did was something for the program and for Coach Williams. We had proven ourselves to all those who doubted Kansas. Those people who said we were too soft, had an easy conference, could not win the big games and whatever other crap they could imagine. Kansas was in the Final 4 and they would have to find a way to deal with it.

Chapter 12

Final Four Week

EUPHORIA

We returned from the victory over Oregon to a state of madness. Kansas was up for grabs and our team had caused the hysteria. We landed at Topeka and were greeted by hundreds of fans cheering, bouncing up and down, holding flowers and cards, handing them to us as we walked through. I was told some of these people had arrived 3 hours earlier, during the final minutes of the game. They wanted to make sure they got a good spot in order to welcome us home.

I had been through crowds before but nothing prepared me for this. The sound of the crowd was different this time. Often you can tell by the tone that there is happiness and support. This crowd had a fervor I had never noticed in the past. These people were earnestly letting us know how they felt about us. It was as though the pitch of voices moved up an octave, from loud to excitedly vocal. They were living a moment many had waited years to experience.

Photo by Earl Richardson

Team thanking the crowd at the NCAA practice site.

The look on their faces was also different. This was not happiness, it was joy. It was the joy of knowing that those once in a lifetime days had arrived. The eyes were dancing and the crinkles on their faces were from sincerity, not forced but honest affection. They loved us and wanted to tell us so.

It hit me in a different way as I walked through the roped off path. Normally I shy away from scenes like this. I don't like being manhandled by crowds of people. This was not the same. I knew this was part of the reward for all the hard work, and it was something I would always remember. I wanted to walk a little slower this time and try and make eye contact with as many people as possible. If I couldn't thank all of them in person, at least I could let a few know how grateful I was for their support.

We got on the bus and looked at one another. Smiles were everywhere along with looks of amazement. I can't think of any guy on that bus who was not moved by the feeling of that crowd. We were all talking and laughing as the bus drove the 20 minutes along I-70 back to Lawrence. Although I knew there would probably be something waiting for us back on campus, I never expected what came next.

The bus dropped us off at Allen Fieldhouse. The number of cars in the surrounding lots gave a hint of what was going to happen. As we entered the doorway, we were directed towards the court and not the locker rooms. The noise level inside became deafening as each player appeared in the doorway. The loudest moment was when Coach Williams walked in. I stood in the center of the court and looked around in a mix of happiness and wonder.

This was the student body and fans who had given me such a mixture of joy and depression over the years. They loved me when I was on the floor. They hounded me as I tried to live a normal day-to-day life. They were critical of me when the team lost or I was in a slump. They were pretty typical of what most college athletes experience in the way of support.

Then I looked closer at the faces. I noticed the eyes of some people and recognized what was there. The same look I had seen only minutes earlier in Topeka was now in the eyes of these fans in our fieldhouse. Something clicked inside my brain. I was finally beginning to understand.

These fans weren't just supporting me. They were letting me know I was part of them. I was a member of their family, a person they cared and felt strongly about. As the cheers increased, I realized this was the only way many of those people could try and reach me. I was not accessible to them on a daily basis and I had tried my best to stay away from many of them. And they didn't care about that or hold it against me. They still wanted to say I love you. They were screaming my name as if to say "I want you to know I'm here for you."

I was overcome with emotion. I felt goosebumps going down my spine and crawling up my arms. My body shook for a second, but it was a sensory reaction, a way to deal with this feeling inside of me. This was going to be the last time I ever stood on the floor of Allen Fieldhouse in front of these fans as a KU basketball player. Whatever we did in the coming week, I would never again be in this spot. If we won, the celebration would be outdoors, due to the number of supporters. If we lost, I still believed there would not be a ceremony in Allen. The number of people who were behind us was as large as the state of Kansas itself.

Now I was looking at things differently. A sense of finality hit me, more than it had on Senior Night. After four years of trying, I and my teammates had nearly reached the top. Kansas was going to the Final Four. It seemed almost unreal to be thinking about that, but it wasn't a dream anymore. It was real and it was spectacular.

I wanted to say some of these things to the crowd. I finally felt comfortable in this setting. I was ready to let them know how I felt about their support and devotion to the team and myself. Somehow the words just couldn't come out. At the moment when I got a chance to speak, I uttered something about how great they were and thanked them for the show of support. But it was not as heartfelt as the feeling I knew was inside of me. I really loved these people. Maybe writing this will let them know how grateful I am for everything.

Downtown Lawrence was awash in KU signs and colors. Nothing in this town escaped the frenzy ignited by the success of the basketball team. Posters were in the windows of every store, signs hung from lampposts, and billboards proclaimed support for Kansas basketball. It was crazy.

The national media descended upon Lawrence. The team was

required to be available to the media for one day, for any press conferences they might want. I got mine done fairly quickly, and thought things might calm down a bit. I was completely wrong.

The phone in my apartment rang continually that week. From 7 a.m. until almost midnight, no more than 10 minutes would go by without a phone call. Nearly all of them were from people who wanted to talk or wish me luck. Later in the week, many of the calls were from girls who wanted to see me or arrange a time to meet. My roommates were a great help to me, fielding all the calls and usually telling people to please not call since I was already gone. By the middle of the week, they were right.

There was no point in staying in Kansas any longer. The attention we were generating would follow us wherever we were, so we might as well be in Atlanta. You have to live through a Final Four week to appreciate how insane the atmosphere becomes. It's as if you are living in a completely unsheltered area. No such thing as privacy exists.

I would not have traded any of this. I had waited my whole career for a week like this and now my team had achieved part of the goal. We were going to the Final Four. We had been rated one of the top four teams the entire season, and we proved everyone correct by making it here. From the start of the new year, we had been either number one, two or three. It was time to finish the argument, to state our case for being the best college basketball team of all.

Sure, it was inconvenient to have the phone ringing nonstop. I was unable to go anywhere in town without being mobbed, so I simply stayed in my apartment or the gym. Even walking out to practice meant going through crowds larger than after some of our home games. Autograph seekers were everywhere. People were constantly calling out my name from crowds.

It was great. I loved it and will always remember that week. Kansas had made it, the talk about our being underachievers was silenced, and I was entering my last few days of college basketball. What a wonderful time.

We flew to Atlanta on Wednesday. The team stayed in a great hotel, separated from the other teams. I flashed back to how things had begun in Maui, how all the teams were gathered for a dinner and those Sony games. It was such a relaxed atmosphere compared to this.

Those games were for a tourney title, but it was a season opener for most teams. They were finding out how good they could be.

We were now at the other end. Kansas was one of four teams who were going to determine who had the absolute best team in America. This tourney was the big one, the only one that matters to most people. The winner of the NCAA is the National Champion. The way we were sequestered bore that out.

The team was put up in the Marriott in Buckhead, a great place to stay. I thought about how I was completing my career by staying in one of the best hotels I had seen during four years at Kansas. This was the last anyone would see of us outside of the Georgia Dome. We stayed in our assigned rooms and this time I had Jeff Carey as my roommate. Seniors together at the end. We had always referred to ourselves as the "old men" of the team. I guess it was logical to put us together now.

Jeff and I talked a lot during the days before the game. We thought it was kind of funny that the two "old vets" as we called ourselves, were rooming together on our last road trip as KU basketball players.

"You think that the coaches planned this?" Carey asked me.

"It wouldn't surprise me. They probably think old farts like us need to get to bed early," I joked.

"You know, this is the last trip we'll take. The guys will never call us the old vets again," he said, getting a bit more serious. His voice sort of drifted off as he finished the sentence and Jeff fell silent for a few moments.

I thought about that. Our careers would be over after these games. Win or lose, this was it.

"Hey, think about all those times when we couldn't wait for practices to end," I said, trying to steer things a different direction. "Remember all the times when we'd hear the word "Sprint" and have to run?"

"Yeah, and I know how much I hated some of those days," Jeff said. "Right now, I thought about something else. I've been here longer than anyone, even you. I'm the true senior member of this team."

"Hey, let's not get too serious here," I suggested. "I can say two words that will make you think of something other than this sad stuff."

"Yeah?"

"Farting machine," I said.

We both broke up immediately, remembering the time Jeff put a farting machine in Michael Lee's locker. It made the sickest sounds, but it was realistic. As Michael walked in to the locker room, Jeff activated the remote. The sound was pretty loud and Michael kept looking at us. Finally he said, 'Man, you are sick. Control yourself." As soon as he turned around, the fart noise went off again. He gave us another look, but we couldn't control our laughter anymore and broke up. We showed him the machine and he thought it was pretty cool.

"Watch me get someone," Michael said, getting an idea. "Hey Drew, come over here," he called out.

Drew Gooden walked over and started to sit down. Jeff made the machine fart again, and Drew jumped back with a disgusted look. "Man, that ain't cool!" he exclaimed. Michael smiled and Jeff let another one rip.

"Damn!" Drew shouted, his voice rising a bit. "You're sick." As he walked away, we all started laughing so hard, we nearly fell off our chairs. Drew figured out he'd been had, and we finally showed him the machine.

"That was one of the great locker room moments," I said to Jeff Carey.

"It's what makes life as a college athlete complete." he said in reply. "We act in such a mature manner."

———————

The first practice was truly unforgettable. We were taken by a bus to the Dome, and dressed in the locker room. We passed Indiana in the hallway on the way to the floor, but nothing was said. I made eye contact with a few of their players and nodded, but that was it. The tone was much more serious than usual. Most of us walked in silence until we got through the tunnel and looked out at the Dome.

The scene was unreal. There must have been at least 20,000 people watching the practices. The crowd was larger than we had for any home game; for that matter, larger than for any regular season game. I thought to myself, "This is crazy. There are too many people here to accomplish anything." It was almost distracting to see so many people at a practice.

Coach Williams must have been thinking as I did. We completed a few drills and ran through some shooting exercises. We went up and down the floor a few times and then shot around. It almost seemed pointless, as if we were only coming out because the

A huge crowd watches the Final Four practice in the Georgia Dome.

networks wanted some footage for their NCAA shows. The only good thing I can say about it was that I now had a feel for how it would be to shoot here. Most arenas are the same, with a few varying backdrops. I had always heard shooting in a Dome would be different. Personally, I didn't see a real problem here.

When the practice was over, Drew and I had to go to the media booth for about 15 minutes of questions. Most of them were the usual type, how did we feel, etc. Then we returned to the locker room and joined the rest of the team with the group press conference. The whole thing was about another half hour in length.

I was a bit surprised to find out how I was reacting to everything in Atlanta. Once we got here, it didn't seem very different from any other tournament at any other level. Sure, the practice was unusual, but that was due to the crowd. As far as nerves or a tense feeling, there was nothing. I felt very relaxed and never really dwelt on this being the Final Four. I had the feeling that people were disappointed when I was asked how I was dealing with the pressure of being at this point. I calmly responded that it was no big deal. That was truly how I felt.

Kansas had drawn the second game against Maryland. Some

people were saying this was the actual title game, since we were the two highest ranked teams left. Going into the tourney, we were ranked #2 and Maryland was #4. It didn't matter who we played by this time. We were only two wins away from the title.

I felt confident. We had played some of our best ball of the year last week, defeating Illinois and Oregon. Going up against Maryland was like playing a team we already knew. Since they were members of the Atlantic Coast Conference (ACC) and their games were always on television, it was as though we had scouted them well. I felt I knew much about how their guards would play. It made me more relaxed and I think my teammates felt the same.

I know that I never thought about the other two teams. At this point, we had focused so much on Maryland that it seemed there would not be any game after this. When you prepare for someone for a week, they become the only important thing in your life. We knew what we had to do and were prepared to do it.

The ride to the Georgia Dome was uneventful. I honestly didn't think it was anything special. As I've said before, these games tend to be the same, and in spite of what you might think, I approached the Final Four game about the same way I had the game against Ball State back in November. I wanted to play basketball and it didn't matter where or against whom. I felt ready to play.

The game against Maryland was a combination of every good and bad sequence we had played all season. The first half saw the patented run, when we simply took off and played the tough defense and high powered transition game that had propelled us to become one of the highest scoring team in America. We were on fire, we seemed to be able to run at will, and they were having trouble keeping up. The score was 13-2 at one point, I was confident and was playing with all the energy I could muster. This was the time to take control of the game.

It's impossible to point to one moment when things changed. Any basketball player can tell you that there are swings in momentum in a game. Opponents will not roll over and play dead when you have a big lead, just as your team won't quit if you're behind. To be the champion, you have to expect these changes and adapt to them. I knew Maryland was not going to let us blow them out of the Final Four, and when they started to come back, I was sure we would adjust and keep control.

We let them get the momentum and then we let them take the lead. By the end of the half Maryland was ahead by 7. That margin put us easily within striking distance, but that wasn't what I wanted. We should have kept the lead, and that's what Coach Dougherty reminded us about at the half.

"After UCLA, I told you guys that you should never let up on an opponent. You can't afford to ever let someone get back into the game, especially a team as good as these guys," Coach Dougherty told us.

Playing defense against Maryland.

He was right. I remembered exactly what he said, because it was something that had bothered me when we lost in January. After that game, Coach Dougherty also added one more statement.

"Sometimes you guys act as though you believe you can turn it on when you want," he said. "If you don't change that way of thinking, there's going to be a game where you won't be able to get the momentum back until it's too late."

I had a feeling this was going to be that kind of game. We had the lead, we had everything going for us, and we let it slip away. However, Maryland was certainly not unbeatable, and we could easily string together another run. It was time for us to do that.

As the team walked out of the locker room, I felt that feeling of confidence again. Looking at who was gathered around our huddle, I saw guys whom I felt were some of the best players in America. Drew, Nick, Kirk and I had been together for three years. I knew as a group, we would take control of things and play with intensity. I believed we'd win this game, but I knew it wouldn't be easy.

Something happened in the second half, something which had not occurred all season. We fell far behind and soon the deficit was an unbelievable 20 points. Drew and Kirk couldn't seem to handle their men defensively, I was not contributing on offense and was not getting open for shots. Nick was about all we had on offense, the other guys were mostly freshmen and things seemed to be falling apart.

This was not the way we planned on playing in the Final Four. It seemed as though we were in a state of total confusion, uncertain as to how we should try to make a comeback. This team always knew how to win. I had the feeling we would figure out what to do before it was too late.

We seemed to regroup and tried to make a final run at Maryland. The team started to get itself back on track with a few selective shots, and then I finally got hot. I hit three straight shots, making an attempt to get the team going again. It suddenly felt as if I couldn't miss, and I knew I was right, that we were going to pull it off, making what would be called an incredible comeback.

It never happened. We let Maryland get too far ahead and there wasn't enough time to catch up. It didn't matter how much we wanted to win this game, Maryland was the better team this night.

The final few minutes were a blur. I remember looking at the clock repeatedly, hoping somehow the time would freeze. Guys were talking, but I only heard voices. It was as though I was in some kind of vacuum, physically in a spot but unable to communicate with others. My career was coming to a close. I would never be a college basketball player again. The dream of playing at Kansas had been achieved. It was now time to wake up and move on with my life.

We came home to another great demonstration of support. The fans had been so intense the previous weeks I wondered how they would be today. I should have known.

Although I knew the fans were sincere in expressing their gratitude towards out efforts throughout the season, the rally seemed hollow to me. We hadn't won the title. I was still disappointed and realizing I'd never get this chance again made it worse. It was kind of hard to go through this with a smile.

The ceremony was held in the football stadium. A stage had been erected at one end of the field. The team, coaching staff, university president and athletic director were all present. We all had a chance to talk to the crowd. After Senior Night and the rally following the game against Oregon, I had the feeling I was becoming a public speaker. The problem for me was that I had run out of anything to say. There was nothing left in me that would get people excited. There was nothing left to say. The season was over.

The highlight, in my mind, came when some Air Force jets flew overhead. The stage seemed to shake from the force of the planes and the noise was intense. The pilots buzzed the crowd and were flying so low you could actually read the writing on their sides. It was extremely impressive.

I watched the NCAA title game in my apartment. My roommates and I bought some sub sandwiches, turned on the television and just sat. Nobody felt like making a lot of comments. The game was pretty uneventful, and the silence in the room made it seem downright dull. I was left with the feeling of an opportunity lost, knowing in my heart that we could and should have been playing in Atlanta that Monday night. I believed then, and will always believe, that we would have defeated Indiana, just as Maryland did that night. It simply wasn't meant to be.

Hitting a three in the final half against Maryland. It turned out to be too little, too late..

Epilogue

People can perceive things as they want them to be. In considering whether or not Kansas has changed during my four years as a starter, I might be guilty of this. Yet, I can't help believe that the team I played upon my senior year was the best of all.

It was unlike any other which Jayhawk fans have admired. The team did not get into things like team meetings. I know that in the past, some teams have held meetings to talk over things. A captain would feel that the team was losing focus or needed motivation and call for a meeting to discuss those problems. I never did that. You have to know the guys you are playing with, and these guys are not the type to talk about problems. We were a team that seemed to sense when we needed to step up and did it. To use a cliche, we let our actions speak louder than our words. I've played with guys through the years who were always telling a team what they needed to start doing. Those same guys were never leading by example. The words would lose their force and end up sounding like empty phrases. Who would care what someone said if they were not doing it themselves?

This was a team that did not worry about things during the season. Again, I know the common wisdom on the outside is that we must have been worried after losing to Ball State, or devastated when we lost to UCLA. People probably thought that when Nebraska almost beat us, we were taking things lightly or starting to doubt how good we were. None of that is true. We were a group of college basketball players. We all knew there will be days when things don't go as planned. It's possible for a team to have a bad shooting night, and it's possible for an opponent to play the game of their lives against us. Having that attitude made us more resilient. We were able to bounce back from bad outings, to shrug off things that might have caused other teams to worry for days.

I would read how the team must have responded to a fiery pep talk or been yelled at due to a poor game performance. Those things were never needed. The Final Four team was not the type to respond to that. We listened when Coach Williams told us what to do. We tried to carry out every game plan. He knew that and he also knew we gave him the best effort within our abilities. Because of that, Coach never needed to give us the impassioned speech people think occurs when a team makes a great comeback. Some basketball players have the desire within themselves and can get themselves motivated in their own manner. This team had individuals like that.

I believe this team had the most ability of the four I played upon at Kansas. The level of talent that Drew Gooden and Nick Collison brought to our front line is incredible. Kirk Hinrich is such a focused and determined person he brings that attitude out in the rest of us. I thought that I added an outside scoring threat and was a steadying influence, the experience factor that is hard to see but recognizable in certain situations. We were fortunate in the fact that our fifth starter, and the guys off the bench came ready to play immediately. Aaron Miles and Keith Langford fit right in, with their personalities and their talent. Wayne Simien, Brett Ballard and Jeff Carey were perfect role players, giving us what we needed at just the right moment. The rest of the guys worked so hard at practice, and played so well during their game appearances, they made everyone better. This team could have been drawn from a textbook on how to assemble a winning basketball team.

I've never played with a more focused or determined group of guys. We had so much desire to win. I believe that was our secret, the one thing outsiders could never have known. Sometimes I wonder if the coaching staff itself knew how badly we wanted to get to the Final Four and win everything. We were a quiet team when it came to things like this. We never talked about goals as a group. There was no rallying cry, yelling before games or at halftimes. We just knew we were going to win. We knew we wanted to win every time we stepped on the floor.

It's hard to explain this to people. Most fans see things in movies or recall how it was when they played sports. Those experiences become reality, those events are how things are always supposed to happen. I guess that means my memories will include the team I played upon. Not much yelling or rah-rah cheering. Instead, an inner force that drives guys to succeed. Sometimes it's called heart. This team had huge hearts, we played a tougher style of basketball than some other Kansas teams because we wanted to.

Even my junior team was accused of not playing tough. Our loss to Illinois in the Sweet 16 game was widely portrayed as Illinois "beating up" on the Jayhawks. We were "soft", we played "finesse", we were "intimidated." All those phrases were thrown in our faces after the game. We lived with that for an entire summer. The sportswriters did us a huge favor by saying these things. I know I was motivated in a different manner because of that. I'd never been called those things before and it pissed me off. I became more aggressive on the floor, especially on defense. I know that Nick Collison took those statements personally, as did many of the other guys. Our games against Stanford and Illinois proved those people wrong, and I knew we would win both games. I knew because we had heart and pride.

The pride factor cannot be underrated. Kansas is one of the best basketball programs in America. Very few schools can match our success. It's something everyone takes as a reflection of themselves. We know we are lucky to be playing here. We know the fans and alumni wear Jayhawk clothing with pride, hoping everyone notices they support Kansas. You don't hide the fact, you advertise it. The guys on the team realize they are a large part of that attitude, and know it's a badge of honor. We never want to be associated with a losing program. I never have been on a losing team. I never will be. I'm a North Dakotan by birth, a Kansas Jayhawk by good fortune and proud to be both things.

It was a long shot for me to make it here. But I did.

About the Author

Mark Horvath has been teaching Economics at Andrean High School for 20 years. He has been a basketball coach at the freshman and junior varsity levels, as well as varsity cross country coach for 15 years. In 1988, Horvath was selected Teacher of the Year for Northwest Indiana by the Inland Steel Company.

In 1997, Horvath co-authored the book "Floor Burns: Inside the Life of a Kansas Jayhawk" with Jerod Haase, former KU standout guard.

Horvath lives in Chicago Heights, Illinois with his wife Nancy and two children, Alison and Andy.

In 2002, Horvath received coach of the year honors for cross country, from the Lake Athletic Conference of N.W. Indiana.